Praise for
The Starbucks Experience

"Yes! Starbucks has changed the way the world experiences coffee, but it has also done so much more— Starbucks has blown the doors off business, marketing, and even popular culture as usual. Dr. Michelli offers keen insights on the transformational power of Starbucks. Better yet, *The Starbucks Experience* makes that power accessible to all of us in business and life!"

—Dr. Jackie Freiberg,
coauthor of *Guts! Companies That Blow the Doors Off
Business as Usual* and *NUTS! Southwest Airlines'
Crazy Recipe for Business and Personal Success*

"This book gives you a series of practical, proven ideas and strategies that you can apply immediately to build a more successful business."

—Brian Tracy,
author of *Million Dollar Habits*

"One of the only things I like better than Starbucks coffee is a great book. In *The Starbucks Experience,* Joseph Michelli has brewed up a stimulating read about Starbucks and how it became a world-class brand. Not only will you get outstanding insights into what makes Starbucks great, but you'll learn how you can use these principles to create a rich experience for your customers as well."

—Mark Sanborn,
author of *The Fred Factor*

"The principles Dr. Michelli reveals have been of immediate value to our fourteen companies. This book is a powerhouse combination of business information *and* insight that will make a difference for you and your organization."

—Scott McKain,
author of *What Customers Really Want,* vice chairman,
Obsidian Enterprises, Inc., and cofounder,
The Value Added Institute

"Starbucks has been a terrific business partner for Johnson Development Corporation. Dr. Michelli offers keen insights into how Starbucks partners, from the store level to corporate leadership, create unique and powerful experiences for staff, customers, and communities. Get this book—make a difference."

—Earvin "Magic" Johnson,
NBA All-Star, chairman and CEO of
Johnson Development Corporation

"The enormous ongoing and on-growing success of Starbucks will make this book of interest to just about everyone. The principles it espouses are dear to my heart, and I recommend it without qualification."

—Ken Blanchard,
coauthor of *The One Minute Manager*®
and *The Secret*

"I know Starbucks! Their first store is just about a block from my business, the World Famous Pike Place Fish Market—you may know us as the guys who throw and catch fish. Dr. Michelli has not only helped me write the story of my business, but in *The Starbucks Experience* he captures the essence of what Starbucks has done to generate unmatched success. Read this book, live the principles, and enjoy profits untold."

—John Yokoyama,
coauthor of *When Fish Fly* and owner of the
World Famous Pike Place Fish Market

"Michelli gives you a practical solution to achieving and sustaining success by creating your unique customer experience."

—Harry Paul,
coauthor of *FISH! A Remarkable Way to Boost Morale and Improve Results* and *REVVED! An Incredible Way to Rev Up Your Workplace and Achieve Amazing Results*

THE STARBUCKS EXPERIENCE

5 Principles for Turning Ordinary into Extraordinary

JOSEPH A. MICHELLI

McGraw-Hill

New York   Chicago   San Francisco   Lisbon   London
Madrid   Mexico City   Milan   New Delhi   San Juan
Seoul   Singapore   Sydney   Toronto

The *McGraw·Hill* Companies

22 23 24 25 DOC/DOC 1 5 4

ISBN-13: 978-0-07-147784-0
ISBN-10: 0-07-147784-5

McGraw-Hill books are available at special quantity discounts to use as premiums and sales promotions, or for use in corporate training programs. For more information, please write to the Director of Special Sales, Professional Publishing, McGraw-Hill, Two Penn Plaza, New York, NY 10121-2298. Or contact your local bookstore.

This book was prepared with the assistance of the Starbucks Coffee Company.

Interior design by Nick Panos.

Printed on acid-free paper.

Library of Congress Cataloging-in-Publication Data

Michelli, Joseph A.
   The Starbucks experience : 5 principles for turning ordinary into extraordinary / by Joseph Michelli.
       p. cm.
   Includes bibliographical references.
   ISBN 0-07-147784-5 (alk. paper)
1. Starbucks Coffee Company. 2. Success in business—Handbooks, manuals, etc. I. Title.
   HD9199.U54S736 2006
   658—dc22   2006016788

contents

foreword

We are litter-picker-uppers. We are green-apron-clad seekers of the book that you might have left on one of the tables in our coffeehouse. We are the folks who smile across the counter at you every morning as you ask for your double-tall-nonfat-mocha-with-a-little-vanilla-at-the-bottom-you-know-my-regular-drink. We're Starbucks partners (commonly known to the world as employees).

I often start stories about our company and culture with a description of us as the litter-picker-upper type of people. We just naturally stoop down to pick up that gum wrapper or soda can on the sidewalk as we're talking with you about how the kids are doing and what crazy weather we're having. It's not a magic formula for hiring or business success; it's just who we are.

Well, maybe it is magic. Because there is something a little magical about founding a business that aspires to enrich the human spirit. That's actually part of the Starbucks core purpose. And we live every day by our Mission Statement and Guiding Principles, which include embracing diversity and creating a great work environment. Sure, one of our principles is to recognize that profitability is essential to our future success. But it's not the first item on the list; it's the last one. And when you live and work according to those kinds of principles, good things seem to come your way.

One of the ways in which we express the nature of what it means to be a Starbucks partner is through the *Green Apron Book*. It's a pocket-sized book that puts into words some of the core "ways of being" that you need in order to be successful at Starbucks. They are *be welcoming, be genuine, be knowledgeable, be considerate,* and *be involved.* They are simple words, and they distill everything you need to know about Starbucks and the people who work here.

We each get to be part of a group that gets to make a huge difference in people's lives in a million small ways—just little moments like smiling as we hand you a drink, hand-crafting your beverage just the way you like it, and providing a comfy chair and a place to get away from it all without going very far.

In my role, I get to travel to hundreds of stores every year to help smooth the road for our store managers and other store partners to provide those experiences for you. I'm all about taking away obstacles and providing tools so that our partners can do what they do best—take care of one another, our customers, and the community. I'm a lucky guy.

And I am also a storyteller. I like to meet and collect stories from our partners and customers, and I find that they are the best way to share the message of our current and future success.

I thought that I had a pretty good collection of stories about Starbucks partners (check out the "pay it forward" story on pages 97–98), but Dr. Michelli uncovered far more than I thought possible! His connection with partners and customers has resulted in a wonderful collection of stories that do more than just help you understand Starbucks; they help you understand the roots of our success and our hopes for the future.

I congratulate Dr. Michelli on hitting on just the right combination of conventional business acumen and storytelling. And the stories you'll find here reveal something that is extremely simple but awe-inspiringly powerful—that people want to do the right thing, they want to create and offer quality things, they want to do good in the world, and if you give them the opportunity and the resources to do so, they will shine. Here's to all the stories that are yet to be told.

JIM ALLING
PRESIDENT, STARBUCKS U.S. BUSINESS

acknowledgments

It seems fitting that I would be writing these acknowledgments in "my Starbucks" on Garden of the Gods Road in Colorado Springs, Colorado, where store manager Mitch Disselkoen and his team consistently create the Starbucks Experience for me. Just as my venti nonfat latte is the result of the efforts of many whose names I will never know (including coffee pickers and farmers a world away), so too is this book the product of gifted and passionate people whose names do not appear on its cover.

The Starbucks Experience is the culmination of nearly two years of collaborative effort that started when I called the customer service number on the back of my Starbucks card. After a little effort and persistence, that number led me to the embodiment of all that is good and right about Starbucks, Chris Gorley of Global Brand Communications. Chris has taken on this project with fervent intensity. She has created opportunities for me at every level of Starbucks, from the president and CEO, Jim Donald, to the baristas behind the counter at the store where I am sitting. Chris's heartfelt respect for her company is matched only by her kindness, competence, and patience.

Throughout this process, Chris teamed up with other amazing Starbucks partners such as Kevin Carothers in Public Affairs and Kelly Sheppard in Public Relations to bring their talents and insights to this work. From the outset, Chris worked closely with Lara Wyss in Media Relations. Lara, along with Dub Hay, senior vice president of Coffee and Global Procurement, and the entire team at the Starbucks Farmers Support Center in Costa Rica, served as guide to my Starbucks Experience on the mountainous coffee farms near San José. Lara's energy, warmth, and sense of humor have been a consistent part of the researching and writing process. From my perspective, if you want to know how Starbucks became the international company it is today, you need only meet Chris and Lara.

The bibliography of this book includes a comprehensive list of the senior leaders at Starbucks who generously took the time to meet with me. I thank each of them for sharing their phenomenal insights on business success. A number of Starbucks managers were particularly helpful in securing contacts and stories for this book. While their own accounts may not be included, their influence was significant. This group includes Tesh Burke, Annette King, and Annette's contacts at the CUP (Caring Unites Partners) fund. The bibliography does not include the names of literally hundreds of customers and partners who have shared information. While space considerations allowed only a subset of the stories I heard to be included in the book, many powerful experiences remain to be written about on another day.

Additionally, I'd like to thank all the CEOs and business leaders who have allowed me to either coach them or provide significant consulting services or programs for their organizations, not the least of which are Dwight Gaudet, Paul

Prouty, Rob Graf, and David Hood. And I want to express my deep appreciation to Dr. Terry Paulson for his incredible mentorship and support.

On the personal side, I have so many people to thank that I will invariably miss some names, but I will never forget each of their contributions. I am in debt to a number of people who got this project off on the right foot. They include Dr. Pat Bernstein, with whom I discussed early ideas for the book, my former personal assistant, Mimi Conwell, and my initial researcher, Mary Pierce. Martha Jewett, my literary agent, not only nurtured this book through its sale to McGraw-Hill, but has also been my confidant, cheerleader, honest critic, and friend. Martha is a voice of inspiration in troubled times. Martha also partnered with my amazing publishing attorney, Lloyd Rich, to ensure that all the legal t's were crossed and the i's were dotted. Donya Dickerson and the great Jeffrey Krames at McGraw-Hill masterfully did what few editors can: they shaped this work and directed it squarely to the market I most wanted to reach. Their timely and insightful comments took this manuscript to the next level.

Countless others have read this book in its various iterations, adding a part to the final product, not the least of which have been Nora Michelli, Heidi Newman, Judy Stenftenagel, Judy Dreis, Alice Manning, and Ruth Mannino. Artistically, the genius of Anthony Landi, Terry Moore, and Heather Sams cannot go unnoticed. Jack Heffron's work on the Reader's Guide reflects his rare talent for turning ideas into learning opportunities. For that, I am thankful.

In truth, this book should reflect the names of two authors. The energy and lifeblood is that of Lynn Stenftenagel. Lynn, my assistant and office manager, has interviewed, researched, edited, rewritten, compiled, cried over, and loved this book. Without her, it would have been a pamphlet, and a meager one at best. I am honored that she let me write it with her.

As always, this book could not have been written without the love and support of my friends and family. I may have written a lot of words in the text, but I can never find the ones to express my gratitude for a God that has given me so much. Nora, we have been through a lot! Thank you for your continued efforts on behalf of the family. You have my deepest and most sincere gratitude for all that you have shared with me during our time together. Fiona and Andrew, I am shutting my computer off now and coming home, but before I do, I lift this cup to everyone who has played a part in *The Starbucks Experience,* and I offer this simple toast of gratitude.

introduction

Taking You and Your Business to the Extraordinary

From its humble origins to a name that is synonymous with coffee, Starbucks is one of the great growth companies of our time. While parts of Starbucks early history have been told in various publications, far too little has been written on precisely how Starbucks revolutionized the coffee industry—and in so doing, rewrote many of the conventional rules of management.

The Starbucks Experience examines the inner workings of a company that has taken an ordinary, even mundane, product and transformed it into extraordinary business success. This inside look at Starbucks has led to the identification of five key principles that are the foundation of Starbucks greatness. These are presented in the chapters that follow—precepts that can truly enhance and expand your business. When applied consistently and with passion, these concepts enable people and companies to seize on the types of opportunities that catapulted Starbucks to its international prominence. But before we get to the "how" of Starbucks, let's consider what Starbucks really has accomplished.

From Seattle to Portland and Beyond

In 1971, the Starbucks Coffee, Tea, and Spice store started business in Seattle, Washington. Before that first Starbucks opened its doors, people stopped by the corner coffee shop for a 50-cent cup that came with the promise of free refills. For some of us, the morning was not complete without a visit to the convenience store, where we poured our own black, murky brew into a white foam cup. To kill the taste, we doused the mixture with gobs of powdered cream and sugar, and stirred it with a thin red plastic stick (which was supposed to double as a straw). We would hand our change to an apathetic cashier who performed the job just well enough to earn the minimum wage. It was an unvarying and uninspired customer ritual and transaction.

Despite the monotonous nature and poor quality of this transaction, most of us didn't know that there was any other way to "enjoy" coffee. While we were slogging through our days with freeze-dried, burnt, or lackluster home-brew, Howard Schultz, Starbucks former CEO and current chairman, asked an intriguing question: "What would happen if you took the quality coffee bean tradition of Starbucks and merged it with the charm and romance of the European coffeehouse?" His answer: Starbucks could transform the traditional American coffee experience from the ordinary to the extraordinary. Of course, it is not clear that even Howard Schultz recognized the huge potential of his vision. Howard disclosed at a Starbucks shareholders' meeting that up to 1980, "Our big dream was to open a store in Portland, Oregon." With over 11,000 stores worldwide, the company has certainly come a long way from its original goal.

By all accounts, Howard's concept was an ambitious idea. How do you change people's view of coffee? After all, coffee has been with us for centuries, and there seemed to be little impetus for a major shift in customers' preferences.

How do you inspire a coffee drinker to give up her regular routine while also getting her to pay six or eight times more for rich, exotic coffee blends when "ordinary" is all she's ever known? Besides, who would make time for a European-style coffeehouse experience when one could grab a cup while buying milk, gasoline, and a newspaper?

Early critics of Schultz's vision maintained that he had happened upon a short-lived gimmick that would quickly fizzle. Others could not grasp what all the fuss was about. As Cora Daniels noted in a *Fortune* magazine article, "The Starbucks story epitomizes 'imagine that' in every sense. When the company went public . . . it had just 165 stores clustered around Seattle and in neighboring states. . . . Skeptics ridiculed the idea of $3 coffee as a West Coast yuppie fad."

Could Howard Schultz's wild "yuppie fad" really work? Clearly he must have been on the right track, for much of the world has embraced his concept of serving gourmet coffee in a relaxed and comfortable environment. In fact, today Starbucks has stores in over 37 countries, averages more than 35 million customer visits each week, and has loyal patrons who typically return 18 times a month. Contrary to the bearish predictions of so-called industry analysts, Starbucks has done fairly well for itself.

What is the true scale of Starbucks success? If you had invested $10,000 in the Starbucks IPO on the Nasdaq in 1992, your investment would be worth approximately $650,000 today. Starbucks has grown substantially faster than the average S&P stock. To get a sense of its profitability, one need only appreciate that since 1992, the value of the S&P rose 200 percent, the Dow 230 percent, the Nasdaq 280 percent, but Starbucks?—5,000 percent! Throughout this period, Starbucks maintained its quality while continuing its aggressive expansion. Today, Starbucks opens five new stores a day, 365 days a year.

Starbucks is more than just a Wall Street Cinderella story. Its culture, brand, and product excellence continue to win glowing accolades. It has been consistently recognized by *Fortune* as one of America's "most admired" companies and best employers. *BusinessWeek* acknowledges Starbucks as one of the best worldwide brands. *Business Ethics* places it on its list of most socially responsible companies each year.

From its original single store, the Starbucks brand has emerged as an unparalleled name that is virtually interchangeable with the word *coffee*. Starbucks has introduced terms like *barista, chai, venti,* and *Frappuccino®* *blended beverage* into our everyday vocabulary. However, the most significant sign that Starbucks has changed not only coffee but our lives is how the stores have affected our neighborhoods and communities. Given the sheer number of retail outlets, it is likely that there is a store within five miles of your home or office, and even more likely that you refer to that store as "my Starbucks." As one loyal customer, Tiffany Tolmen, puts it, "I actually know where all the Starbucks are in my town, and I literally give directions to my friends using Starbucks as my landmark." Not only has Starbucks changed business, but it has also changed American culture and affected culture worldwide.

Why This Book?

Clearly, Starbucks has grown from humble beginnings and is a "grande" success story based on Howard Schultz's original vision. But doesn't that describe the vast majority of successful businesses? A vision and a plan executed to perfection are what characterize great businesses. However, we are not talking about most businesses. Starbucks is one of the truly exceptional American success stories, a company that so dominates its market that there isn't even a close second. What fuels its incredible growth engine?

Like many in the business community, I've long been mesmerized by Starbucks. Time and again, I have found myself asking: How does the company do that? What do its managers know that managers in other industries could learn? How can Starbucks have two successful stores literally across the street from each other?

In contrast to McDonald's—another great American success story—Starbucks is not a franchise business. So how can it continue to open so many stores from Seattle to Singapore and not cannibalize its own sales? How does Starbucks continue to grow and innovate, while maintaining the consistency and warmth of its first store in Seattle's Pike Place Market? And, most important, what are the lessons to be gleaned from Starbucks that can be applied to other businesses and industries? What are the key success principles that will help any manager take his or her business to the next level?

I decided to approach Starbucks senior management personnel to secure their cooperation on a book project and was surprised when the managers agreed to let me look closely into their organization. While at first I was amazed by the grace, openness, and free rein they gave me, I later came to learn how much their willingness to grant me access was at the core of their success model.

As Jim Alling, president of Starbucks U.S. Business, notes in the foreword to this book, the accomplishments of Starbucks leadership are not the result of magic. Instead, they are driven by a powerful passion for product, people, experience, and community. Every day this passion comes to life in nearly every corner of the world, in an amazing mix of principled behavior that those in the company refer to as the *Starbucks Experience*.

The Starbucks Experience can be found on two very distinct levels in the company:

1. *In its unique corporate culture.* Leaders within the business create a unique culture for employees in which empowerment, entrepreneurship, quality, and service define the values of the firm.

2. *In its passing down of these values to its partners.* The partners, in turn, help create a unique and personal experience for customers. Understanding these principles and getting to know how Starbucks leadership and partners (the term Starbucks uses for all its employees) have grown the company offers a powerful blueprint for transforming your ordinary into your extraordinary.

Share the Wealth: Start with the Experience You Create for Your People

Starbucks has achieved its award-winning corporate culture in large part through the moves and decisions made by Howard Schultz and his leadership team. For any organization, it's difficult, albeit not impossible, to soar with the eagles if you are led by a flock of turkeys. And at Starbucks, the leadership has focused on creating a culture in which employees can soar.

In an article for *Workforce Management,* writer Samuel Greengard pointed out,

> *Starbucks Corporation went public in June 1992. On the first day of trading, the stock closed at $21.50—up from an opening price of $17. Not only did the CEO's net worth zoom; the coffee retailer had finally reached the big leagues. But instead of hoarding his beans, Schultz decided that he would give some of them back to employees in the form of stock options. . . . [While] other firms offered options only to key senior executives, Schultz made them available to everyone working 20 hours a week or more, including those standing behind the counter at a local Starbucks store.*

So why did Howard Schultz and Starbucks leadership take this unconventional approach? According to Geoff Kirbyson in a brandchannel article, Howard noted, "The way we have built our company by including the success of the company with everyone in it and not leaving our people behind is a great example of building a business the right way." From Starbucks perspective, that "right way" to conduct business means truly turning employees into partners—shareholders with a stake in the outcome of the company.

Starbucks leadership offers a refreshing philosophy in a time when many CEOs pocket millions while leaving their employees' pension funds insolvent. Starbucks executives continue to respectfully and willingly share profits with their people. Through this sharing, partners appreciate the direct link between their effort and the success of the business enterprise.

The importance of this shared gain is reflected in conversations with individuals like Omollo Gaya, a Starbucks partner who immigrated to the United States from Kenya. While

7

standing in a coffee-tasting room at the Starbucks Support Center in Seattle, Omollo shared, "I cashed in my Starbucks stock options after six years, and took the $25,000 profit to build a new four-bedroom house for my mother, who is a widow. This is my company. I am an owner, and I am responsible for creating greatness here, just as my treatment has been great." Starbucks profitability has been good for Omollo, and reciprocally Omollo's passion and sense of responsibility benefit the business.

Many managers and business leaders don't talk to their employees about the importance of profit. It is as if "profitability" were a dirty word or a concern that is outside the interests of workers. By contrast, Starbucks leadership has done an exceptional job of both linking a partner's financial gain to Starbucks profit and helping partners understand that profit is the lifeblood of business. Even the Starbucks mission statement acknowledges that partners need to commit to "profitability [which] is essential to our future success." Profits increase not only the breadth of Starbucks market, but also the scope of its positive social influence and its capacity to provide quality benefits for partners. These benefits include health insurance for 20-hours-per-week employees, something that Starbucks partners received long before such a thing was even considered, let alone adopted, by other corporations.

But the treatment that partners receive at Starbucks goes well beyond stock options and health insurance. For example, partners are given extensive training in product knowledge, guiding principles for success, personal empowerment, and the importance of creating warm customer experiences. In stunning contrast to most Fortune 500 companies, Starbucks consistently spends more on training than it does on advertising.

That training pays huge dividends for Starbucks in retaining employees, maintaining connections with current customers, and bringing new customers into its stores. Starbucks staff retention is unprecedented in the quick-service restaurant sector. The employee turnover rate at Starbucks, according to some reports, is 120 percent less than the industry average. Maryann Hammers states in *Workforce Management,* "Starbucks employees have an 82% job-satisfaction rate, according to a Hewitt Associates Starbucks Partner View Survey. This compares to a 50% satisfaction rate for all employers and 74% for Hewitt's 'Best Place to Work' employers."

While not every leadership team can reward employees with stock options or health-care benefits for part-time employees, every business leader can treat those individuals with enough daily care and concern to inspire passion and creativity in their work.

In its mission statement, Starbucks leadership has committed to "provide a great work environment and treat each other with respect and dignity." As with all aspects of its mission, Starbucks management has established internal checks to make sure that leaders are actually living the company's espoused values. This process encourages all partners to bring their concerns to a Mission Review Committee when they feel that policies, procedures, or leadership behaviors are straying from Starbucks commitments.

One such concern involved the lack of paid leave for adoptive parents. Within three weeks of this issue making its way to the Mission Review Committee, Starbucks leadership provided this parent group a two-week benefit. If leaders expect staff to meet and exceed the expectations of their customers, those same leaders must respond to concerns and exceed expectations on behalf of their staff.

As Starbucks International president Martin Coles suggests, "There needs to be cultural alignment between the partners and Starbucks itself. I think it's important within the company that, as leaders, we're the first ones who have to live the principles and the values of the company, because it's impossible to ask our people to behave the same way if we're not willing to go down that track ourselves. The mission statement, the principles, and the behaviors laid out as ways of being are not programmatic. They are just the way you live your life. That is very difficult to fake. Ultimately the organization will self-select, in a way, toward a group of partners who are like-minded."

Martin goes on to indicate that creating this "like-minded" vision of a positive, team-oriented workforce does not occur by accident. "We've spent a lot of time with our partners, both in the selection process and in helping them understand what we stand for as individuals, and what the company stands for as a whole, and the difference we intend to make." It is by design, not default, that Starbucks leadership creates a powerful experience for its partners. It is expected that partners will pass on the dignity and respect that they are afforded into interactions with their customers.

Starbucks partner Joy Wilson suggests that this approach is working. "One of the reasons that Starbucks employees are often so pleasant and helpful is that Starbucks is a great company to work for. It takes care of employees and treats us with respect. That mind-set trickles down from the executives to the thousands of baristas worldwide. I have worked in horrible places, and it's hard to do a good job when you hate the company. We're encouraged to have a good time while we're at work, and that makes a huge difference in the atmosphere we create for the customers."

Paul Williams of Idea Sandbox, a former Starbucks partner and currently a consultant who works with Starbucks, puts it this way: "Starbucks is a human company. That's the difference there. The mission statement and the intentions—they're not just on paper. They truly are meant to be the way things get done. The biggest story at Starbucks is that it's as much about people as it is about coffee."

The respect that leadership offers the employees is also often reflected in the way in which employees respect and create an experience for one another. John Moore, the founder of Brand Autopsy Marketing Practice and a former partner with Starbucks, notes, "What I truly found special about the store experience was that it was basically a family. What leadership offered to us, we offered to one another." Leaders who treat their staff with respect encourage their employees to do the same for their coworkers.

Creating the Starbucks Experience for Customers

Starbucks management takes pride in the company being "the leading retailer, roaster and brand of specialty coffee in the world," but also recognizes that people flock to the company's stores for the total Starbucks Experience. In essence, people come into a comfortable setting where they are valued on a personal level, and where a meaningful connection is made. Everything the company does is intended to give the customer a positive, perhaps uplifting, experience while purchasing a quality beverage or food item.

To achieve this, the ambience of the store must be inviting; the store must be a place where a person will feel comfortable hanging out alone or with friends. This setting, often referred to by Starbucks partners as the "third place," must capture a unique warmth that sets it apart from the first two places in most people's lives: work and home.

Customers must be able to customize their beverage order, with the handcrafted assistance of their *barista* (the Italian word for bartender and the term used at Starbucks for a coffee preparer). Customization means satisfying each customer's unique expectations, and often involves special temperatures, soy milk, and various pumps of flavor. It is not uncommon to hear customized orders for drinks as complicated as "quad, two-pump vanilla, one and one-quarter pumps sugar-free hazelnut, ristretto latte, with one-quarter soy, one-half nonfat, one-quarter organic milk, extra hot, with three ice cubes and whip." Such an order is but one part of the richness of the personalized Starbucks Experience.

While seemingly endless details go into producing the emotional bond that loyal Starbucks customers feel, often the most important aspect of this bond is the personal investment of Starbucks partners. As Howard Schultz noted on brand channel.com,

> *The success of Starbucks demonstrates . . . that we have built an emotional connection with our customers. . . . We have a competitive advantage over classic brands in that every day we touch and interact with our customers directly. Our product is not sitting on a supermarket shelf like a can of soda. Our people have done a wonderful job of knowing your drink, your name, [and] your kids' names.*

Starbucks executives and managers alike understand the importance of this personal connection. Leadership spends a great deal of time helping partners seize opportunities to positively affect the lives of those they serve, and in so doing build the brand.

When staff members understand how their efforts spark the business and uplift and change lives, they are more likely to exert the creative and passionate energy that gets noticed by customers. Seth Godin, the author of *Purple Cow: Transform Your Business by Being Remarkable,* describes the difference he observed between Starbucks staff and the staff from a similar retail establishment. As Seth was heading toward a Starbucks store, he overheard two young people from a nearby fast-food restaurant complaining in detail about their jobs. By contrast, upon entering Starbucks, Seth "noticed, tucked deep in the corner, apparently not for customer inspection, a bulletin board. It was jammed with pictures of the staff. The staff on a picnic, at an amusement park, kidding around . . . if it's possible to make an herbal tea with enthusiasm, they were doing it. If it's possible to make a $4 transaction feel joyful, they accomplished it."

Seth relates how soundly and authentically the partners in that Starbucks had "made the store their own." As he puts it, the staff chose to find enjoyment in their jobs. "It was helping not just Starbucks, but them, too. All I had to do was glance out the window to see the difference. I think there's a huge lesson here. Not just for marketers who sell interactions . . . but for employees, as well." That huge lesson is the Starbucks Experience—a commitment to the shared good of all employees and customers. It happens by creating systems to hold leadership and staff accountable for that commitment, sharing the reward of hard work, and encouraging profitability. By projecting a vision of the optimal customer experience and helping partners consistently realize that vision, Starbucks leaders watch their people grow the business, and watch their profits grow as well.

Staying Vigilant

Despite the company's success, Starbucks leaders understand their current and future vulnerabilities. For example, the larger Starbucks grows, the harder it will be to foster the unique Starbucks Experience. To put it simply, in the words of Howard Schultz, Starbucks has to work to "stay small while growing big." To that end, the future of Starbucks lies in its partners owning millions of positive daily interactions throughout the company.

Anne Ewing, director of Development, Midwest, declares: "Coffee is this amazing agricultural product that is our vehicle to start the conversation with the customer. It happens to be our bridge. Coffee has a life of its own and a rich history, and we get to deliver it. But at the end of the day, our success is linked to the nuances in the store that add up to something special. We must be vigilant about so many things: our design, how our partners feel when they put on their green aprons, and creating a special place for our people to work and our customers to visit."

For Starbucks management, the creation of "special" customer interactions is an extraordinary challenge. Starbucks workforce has grown exponentially, from 100 in 1987 to more than 100,000 in 2006. Given Starbucks rapid and aggressive growth, its leadership faces the challenge of attracting quality people and training them in the Starbucks way, all the while sustaining a culture in which employees excel at connecting with patrons. It is almost like a giant juggling act in the midst of a bustling midway, and every so often, one of the company's balls drops to the ground. But that's the cost of admission for a huge growth engine like Starbucks. Senior management, while never falling into the trap of complacency, is secure in the knowledge that the company has an edge. Its unique culture, the intimacy of its brand, and the uniqueness of the customer experience will keep people coming back.

Dave Olson, senior vice president of Culture and Leadership Development, put it well when he said, "It doesn't matter how many millions or billions of cups of coffee Starbucks serves, if the one you get doesn't suit you. Starbucks has to be able to perform at that level of consistency for the individual automatically, and that's really the promise. We will deliver a drink that suits you every time—and create an experience in the process! The experience must fit the customer."

While in some companies the sincerity of such a statement might be questioned, at Starbucks, concrete examples of understanding the customer can be identified at all levels. Partners consistently seek new ways to fill customers' needs.

Barista Francine Brodeur from Ontario, Canada, shares how "we are empowered to make each customer's visit count. Every now and then, a customer will return within a few minutes of ordering, and order again. Following a quick, hopefully well-placed comment, it comes out that the customer has spilled his drink before fully enjoying it. Sometimes he is obviously 'marked' by the experience, and we offer assistance. That is when I let the customer reorder the same drink; then I tell him that it's on us, since we don't expect payment for the one that got away. The customer is always surprised and tries to pay anyway, to no avail. What makes me proud to work for this company is that I can take liberties to make things right." Francine's comments reflect the satisfaction of customers and Starbucks partners. They help us understand the benefits that emerge when a company gives the human connection a priority commensurate with that of product and service quality.

The Experience That Is Starbucks

As an outsider with no personal stake in Starbucks future, I am *not* here to sell you on the company. It has done an excellent job of promotion worldwide, without help from business authors. I also am *not* here to convince you that Starbucks is one of the best global business enterprises. Many others, who are more knowledgeable than I, have drawn that conclusion. Instead, the key to this book is to offer insights into the unique Starbucks Experience. It is an experience that has an impact on the coffee industry, the broader business world, the environment, partners, customers, and communities from Seattle, Washington, to Darjeeling, India.

From my 18-month exploration into the world of Starbucks, listening to what Starbucks leaders say and watching what they do, I have derived five key business principles that drive its phenomenal success. These principles are offered in the hope that you will apply them to your own situation to enrich your leadership influence in business and beyond. The Starbucks Experience reflects tenets that are simple, yet not simplistic. They are results-oriented and can be deceptively powerful when applied:

1. Make it your own

2. Everything matters

3. Surprise and delight

4. Embrace resistance

5. Leave your mark

The impact of these principles transcends the Starbucks story and offers all business leaders an opportunity to greatly enrich their workplace. They demonstrate how an entrepreneurial spirit and extraordinary leadership skills can elevate a product or service and even change the way in which that product or service is delivered. These guidelines allow each of us to improve our workplace, whether by developing appealing new products, opening new markets, or just paying attention to the aspects of our business that we can readily enhance.

In the spirit of Starbucks, these principles encourage us to listen and respond with a greater awareness of opportunity. They remind all of us—you, me, the janitor, and the CEO—that we are responsible for unleashing a passion that ripples outward from behind the scenes, through the customer experience, and ultimately out into our communities. Let's take a closer look at each of these principles with an eye to how they work inside Starbucks and how we can tap into their transformational power.

make it your own

"This is the true joy of life, the being used up for a purpose recognized by yourself as a mighty one; being a force of nature instead of a feverish, selfish little clot of ailments and grievances, complaining that the world will not devote itself to making you happy."

—GEORGE BERNARD SHAW

Material Ownership versus Making It Your Own

Business leaders today want their employees to be fully engaged in their work rather than simply going through the motions. Often employees do not see how their efforts help the organization succeed. Similarly, employees cannot see how the business's success relates to them. When this type of disconnect exists, it is usually because senior management has failed to demonstrate to staff members the constructive impact they have on those they serve.

Like most companies, Starbucks has wrestled with ways to invite its partners to fully engage their passions and talents every day in every interaction at work. Simultaneously, the leadership has to ensure that individual partners' differences are blended into a generally uniform experience for customers.

Finding a balance between these two important, yet sometimes divergent, leadership responsibilities can be awkward. Yet through its principle of Make It Your Own, Starbucks has succeeded in creating a unique model that encourages partners at all levels to pour their creative energy and dedication into everything they do.

No manager can tell employees how to bring out their individuality while functioning effectively in accordance with the business's priorities; no scripted customer service approach can make this happen. But leaders at Starbucks have provided a structure that allows partners to infuse themselves into their work, so that they can inspire customers in legendary ways. The leaders call this the "Five Ways of Being":

- Be welcoming

- Be genuine

- Be considerate

- Be knowledgeable

- Be involved

To reinforce these concepts, Starbucks management developed a pamphlet that fits neatly into a partner's apron pocket and is appropriately referred to as the *Green Apron Book.* This book offers concrete ideas on how to personalize relationships with customers by giving to, connecting with, and elevating customer interactions.

In an article for Tom Brown's bankstocks.com, David M. Martin, chief training consultant of NCBS, an industry leader in retail banking solutions worldwide, states that the *Green Apron Book,* along with Starbucks Five Ways of Being, "truly encapsulates the core philosophies of Starbucks. Cover to cover, it may take five minutes to read . . . and that's if you pause to sip your coffee a few times. Think about it. In essence, the company is *marketing to its employees* how important the principles and philosophies contained in this book are."

David notes that Starbucks leadership has built an optimistic message into the book: "Instead of overwhelming folks with reams of minutiae and too-rigid instructions, it gives guiding principles of the environments they hope to create and legendary service they strive to provide." This is leadership at its best: simple instruction provided in an appealing way, with a spirit that offers hope.

Since you probably don't have a green apron, let alone a *Green Apron Book*, let's take a look at how Starbucks guides its staff members into making the Starbucks Experience uniquely their own.

Be Welcoming

While most individuals would not think of inviting guests into their home, only to ignore them, many business leaders fail to make their companies equally inviting. At Starbucks, "being welcoming" is an essential way to get the customer's visit off to a positive start. It is also the foundation for producing a predictably warm and comfortable environment. It enables partners to forge a bond with customers so that infrequent visitors become regulars, many of whom end up customers for life.

Many important customer questions are answered in the first moments of a business interaction. Do the staff members care to get to know me? Do they remember me? Will they take care of my needs? Do I matter? Am I invisible?

Starbucks management recognizes that these are key concerns for every person with whom the company does business. The leadership emphasizes the creation of a welcoming experience precisely to let customers know that they are important. According to Starbucks International president Martin Coles, "People want to be recognized. They want to be celebrated in some way. They want to be made to feel as if they really do count for something. And they want a place where they can belong in the community that stands for something more than just an enterprise that makes money. The thing in our company and the thing that works universally is this whole notion of Third Place. It's about the in-store experience—all of it."

At its essence, Starbucks management defines *be welcoming* as "offering everyone a sense of belonging." The leaders emphasize that partners can and should use their individual talents and knowledge to create a place where people feel that they are a priority and where their day can be brightened, at least for a moment. This experience is what most customers seek from Starbucks. Therefore, the leaders expect that customers will consistently be welcomed at all locations, with the partners fully engaged in making that happen. With this expectation in mind, the leaders encourage partners to use their own unique style to produce inviting encounters.

What's in a Name?

Welcoming people by name and remembering them from visit to visit is a small thing, but it counts. The great Dale Carnegie recognized this in his book *How to Win Friends and Influence People*. Carnegie remarked, "Remember that a person's name is to that person the sweetest and most important sound in any language." Carnegie even suggested that a person's name may be his or her most valuable possession.

Barista Joy Wilson shows what is possible when staff members put their own individual style into being welcoming, "I'm the drive-through queen at my store. I always set out to do the best job I possibly can. One of the ways I do that is I learn people's names and drinks and the name of their dog and where their kids go to school and whatever else I can find out about them."

Joy is serious about knowing customers' names. In fact, after work she enters information about her customers into a spreadsheet, which she later reviews. Starbucks leaders helped Joy appreciate the importance of being welcoming and praised her approach. They do not expect or encourage others to use Joy's method. Instead, the leaders provide partners with the freedom to find what works best for them, their customers, and their stores. And it's through leadership's guidance, encouragement, and acceptance of their uniqueness that partners generate new ways to excel.

23

Acknowledging Uniqueness

When someone actually notices us, as Joy notices her customers, it's almost shocking, particularly if we haven't visited that business in a while. In today's frantic world, most of us expect to just blend in with the crowd. Unfortunately, as much as each of us may want to stand out, we often fear that we are just another member of the herd.

Starbucks leadership understands that customers long to have their uniqueness recognized. Therefore, these leaders impart the importance of treating people in a way that leaves everyone feeling unique and special—whether they are customers, clients, or staff members. Paul Ark in Bangkok provides a perfect example of how a Starbucks partner made him feel truly important. A self-proclaimed "sucker" for Frappuccino® blended beverage with raspberry syrup, Paul hadn't been to the Chidlom Starbucks in almost two months, but as he was standing behind two other customers in line to order, one of the baristas looked over and said, "Grande Vanilla Crème Frappuccino® with raspberry syrup, right?"

Paul was shocked, but the experience made a deep impression on him. As he notes, "Most companies chant 'customer service' like some mantra, as if printing it enough times in their corporate glossies means they are actually paying more than lip service to the concept. But here is a Joe Schmo line worker at Starbucks defining what customer service means in real terms to real customers: building a one-on-one rapport in order to remember a customer's needs and preferences and creating a smooth and efficient in-store experience."

Successful business leaders emphasize, train, and encourage a respect for the discretion and uniqueness of their staff. At Starbucks, that discretion comes in the form of giving priority to being welcoming, demonstrating generally what being welcoming looks like, refreshing that image, and then letting people make that concept their own as they bring it into the lives of those they serve.

Create Your Own Experience

- Is your business giving your customers those memorable welcomes?

- How can you help your team members bring their unique brand of welcoming to your business?

- Look around. Whom can you welcome today?

Be Genuine

Starbucks leadership helps partners embrace the idea of being genuine and the importance of that idea to the Starbucks Experience. The concept of what it takes to be genuine is fairly straightforward, but profound. At Starbucks, being genuine means to "connect, discover, and respond." Focusing on these three elements in each customer interaction forms a quality relationship. By contrast, how many of us have been served by people who gave the impression that they couldn't have cared less?

Customers aren't looking for best friends; they just want a positive connection, and they want their needs to matter. They resent being treated as if they were just wallets with humans attached. In order for a connection to occur, a person has to feel heard. Genuineness requires listening through both verbal and nonverbal channels.

It is through this listening that baristas like Angela anticipate the needs of their customers. Angela recalls, "It was Saturday, and this poor woman who was just an emotional
wreck came through. It was her first visit. Our menu can be
a little intimidating, so she stared and then ordered just a
plain coffee. When we asked her if she was sure she didn't
want to try something else, she explained that she was con-
fused and overwhelmed, and she looked like she was about
to cry. In the meantime, we had someone make a Toffee Nut
Latte, because who doesn't like that? We said, forget the plain
coffee; we made you this Toffee Nut Latte—on the house
today for you to try. She was thrilled! She drove off, and we
didn't think much of it other than that we were happy to have
made her happy."

But the story gets better, as Angela explains. "A couple of
days later, we got flowers sent to our store thanking us for
'saving her life.' Her letter explained that she had been having a really, really bad day. After she had visited our store,
she had a piece of joy in her and was able to take care of her
problems and even help someone else to feel better. She is
now one of our regulars."

Angela and her colleagues took the initiative to create an
experience for a customer that was well beyond anything that
the customer could have expressed. That's being genuine and
making the business your own.

Expectations and Service: Connect

Legendary service comes from a genuine desire and effort to
exceed what the customer expects. Repeatedly, customers
have shared experiences of Starbucks partners doing the
extraordinary—making a connection well beyond some for-
mulaic greeting. Take Lydia Moore from Oakland, Califor-

nia, for example. Lydia met the love of her life in Starbucks. While that meeting alone created a special connection to the coffee shop for Lydia, partners strengthened that connection in genuine ways.

Lydia reports that she felt the staff cared about her, and so she kept them posted on the development of her relationship and her engagement. Lydia says, "When we went back and told the two clerks at Starbucks, they were so excited! They put our picture up on the board, and we were like celebrities at that store."

Lydia invited the partners to her wedding, and they, in turn, donated coffee for her special event. Unfortunately, in the first year of their marriage, Lydia's husband was diagnosed with cancer. Starbucks again served as an important connection: "While he was in treatment, in and out of the hospital, there were only two things he wanted—his Grande Drip and his Hazelnut Sticky Bun." Lydia's husband died just after their first anniversary. Lydia recalls, "When he passed away, I was devastated. Amazingly, the clerks from Starbucks came to the funeral, and you could see that they were genuinely affected by the loss."

Who wants to get connected and have to feel the roller coaster of emotions that comes with that? In many businesses, connections never happen. It's simply a matter of transactions. Then again, what's the value to customers if a service business offers only bland, sterile service? And why would employees want to participate in such empty exchanges? Ultimately, by connecting on a personal level, both customers and employees find enhanced meaning in ordinary moments.

When it comes to the ability of human contact to enhance a product, Howard Schultz, in an interview with *Know*™, put it this way:

We are not in the coffee business serving people, but in the people business serving coffee. The equity of the Starbucks brand is the humanity and intimacy of what goes on in the communities. . . . We continually are reminded of the powerful need and desire for human contact and for community, which is a new, powerful force in determining consumer choices. . . . The Starbucks environment has become as important as the coffee itself.

True leaders, in other words, show staff that their individual uniqueness gives them a special way to connect with others.

Discover

28

While listening is critical to creating a connection, business success requires the discovery of each customer's needs and individual situation. In a strange way, the customer relationship begins the same way a romantic relationship does—by seeking an understanding of another person's wants and desires. Sadly, many relationships (both customer and romantic) come to an end simply because one or both parties stop their process of discovery.

While customer service isn't about romance, Starbucks understands that discovery is essential to developing a unique and genuine bond. It is through inquiry that we find out the special qualities of all customers and sometimes help them gain an awareness of needs that even *they* didn't know they had.

Susan, a barista in Ohio, comments, "We get people who come into my Starbucks store to browse our merchandise. I love selling coffee machines because I know I can get behind our product. I've learned everything I can about all our machines, and I pair people up with the right one. I use the 'connect, discover, respond' model. I typically ask, 'Are you brewing it just for yourself? Because then a French Press might be great. If you need to brew 12 cups of coffee at once, then we've got our Starbucks Barista Aroma Grande™.' It's amazing how appreciative people are when you help them get their needs met."

Respond

While a lot of businesses actually do connect with their customers and discover those customers' needs, they don't always act on what they learn. They are long on interest and short on effort to address the customer's actual need. Customers feel betrayed when they are lured into believing that their input matters, only to find out that their preferences are ignored. Starbucks partners are trained not just to listen to their customers, but to take action immediately based on what they hear, and to learn from these experiences for future customer interactions.

Betty Doria from Middle Island, New York, reinforces this concept. Betty and her husband were traveling through Tennessee when they "made a wrong turn and accidentally found a Starbucks. There was a sign in the store for coffee with malt. Real malt! I got so excited because I hadn't seen anything like that since I was a kid in Brooklyn. I got to talking with the manager and started to tell her about how they made real malteds back then." However, says Betty, the manager "made my coffee with malt, and it wasn't that great." But instead of ignoring the customer's dissatisfaction, this manager listened to Betty and worked with her to make the drink

29

to Betty's taste. Listening followed by action—those were the essential ingredients for the success of Betty's experience and the experiences of all customers and staff alike.

Connect, discover, and respond. Each of us can incorporate those elements into our relationships—with peers, supervisors, subordinates, and customers.

Create Your Own Experience

- What are you doing to encourage the discovery of the unique needs of those whom you and your colleagues serve?

- What can you do to invest more of yourself and to get others to invest more of themselves in the process of interpersonal connection and discovery?

- Are you taking action and following through on those discoveries?

Be Considerate

Starbucks leadership challenges partners to be considerate of needs on a global level, and staff members consistently deliver on this challenge. By making consideration their own, Starbucks partners look beyond their own needs and consider the needs of others. In this context, "others" includes a large cast of characters: customers, potential customers, critics, coworkers, other shareholders, managers, support staff, farmers, those who pick the coffee beans, vendors, and even the environment. In essence, "others" equals the entire universe of people and things that Starbucks and its products affect.

For Starbucks, at the corporate level, "being considerate" means exploring the long-term well-being of partners and those individuals whose lives the partners touch, all the while being mindful of the earth's ability to sustain the demands that Starbucks places on it. Specifically, it means things like Starbucks exploration of alternative and renewable energy options. As a meaningful first step, Starbucks leadership is replacing 5 percent of the energy used in its U.S. company-operated stores with wind energy. It is also reducing carbon dioxide emissions by 2 percent. These actions are occurring despite the fact that wind energy now costs about double what coal energy does. Through these choices, Starbucks management proves that thoughtfulness isn't an immediate way to raise profits, but rather a long-term means for survival and prosperity.

The company demonstrates being globally considerate in many ways. As part of the acquisition of Ethos Water, Starbucks leaders set a goal of providing $10 million to water projects in developing countries over the next five years. Ethos was founded in 2002 on the premise that the sale of bottled water could help ensure clean water supplies for children around the world. Every time Starbucks sells a bottle of Ethos™ water, it supplies 5 cents for worldwide water projects. The list of Starbucks social considerations, taken at the corporate level, is daunting and includes everything from building schools and health clinics to supporting coffee farms and ensuring quality conditions for migrant coffee pickers.

Not only does the *be considerate* approach strengthen the environment and the company's suppliers, but it has a profound effect by showing all partners what can be accomplished through a farsighted, other-oriented approach.

31

At the store level, partners are constantly finding ways to be considerate in terms of local environmental and social issues. Stefanie Harms explains how thoughtfulness can be directed toward the community: "It was National Tree Day in Australia, and a bunch of partners from Victoria gave up their time to meet at Burnley Park to plant trees with other volunteers. For me, it was a fun day on which I got to observe the spirit and camaraderie that exists among Starbucks partners. To my left, there were partners up to their elbows in mud, planting trees and chatting with families from the area, and to my right, there were Rohan and Celeste handing out free drip coffee to volunteers on a break, chatting proudly about the Fair Trade Certified™ Timor Lorosae coffee samples." Stefanie and her teammates demonstrate what can be accomplished both personally and socially when leaders encourage their staff members to make environmental and community service their own.

Looking Within

A sense of community—and respect for one another—is increasingly rare in the modern workplace. Coworkers frequently treat one another far worse than they do customers. Considerate actions taken by leadership can serve to encourage thoughtful and respectful behavior among staff members.

When thoughtfulness becomes a part of a company's culture, amazing acts of selflessness occur, and the lives of all are enriched. For example, Mary Champaine was a manager at a Starbucks Urban Coffee Opportunity store, a store run through a joint venture partnership with Johnson Development Corporation as a vehicle for economic development in financially challenged neighborhoods.

Mary had gone through more than her own share of personal adversity. Her son was killed in a violent crime, and her husband died of cancer. Also, before going to work for Starbucks, she had lost her previous job at a company that had gone bankrupt. However, despite all this personal turmoil, Mary had a remarkable commitment to her Starbucks team and her store. During a bus strike in Los Angeles, she was known to pick up staff members and bring them to work. In the spirit of being welcoming and being genuine, her pickup service extended to regular customers as well.

Having noticed that the California lottery jackpot had swelled to $87 million, Mary talked to her staff about buying tickets and collected $1 from each employee except two who weren't working. According to an article in the Associated Press, Mary conveyed, "I just went down in my purse and I found enough change to include everybody. We are a team here."

Incredibly, Mary won the jackpot. She had the legal right under California law to claim all $87 million for herself. But, to the surprise of almost everyone except Mary, she decided to share her winnings equally! In an interview aired on CNN, Mary reflected: "We here at Starbucks work as a team, and we support one another. And if I would have taken all the money, then I wouldn't have been part of the team, and everything that I've been working for would be nothing."

Most acts of consideration at work don't have such extraordinary endings, but they certainly can when leadership places a priority on consideration and when leaders encourage staff members to put their own twist on the concept. It is in this leadership environment that the ordinary often is transformed into the extraordinary.

33

Be Knowledgeable

When Starbucks leaders ask partners to "be knowledgeable," they are encouraging employees to "love what they do and share it with others." In the information age, no matter what we do for a living, we add value to our efforts when we gain work-related knowledge. More important, as we become more informed, our value to the business, our self-confidence, and the real impact we have on others all increase.

Not only do Starbucks managers encourage partners to enhance their expertise in the areas of coffee and customer service, but the leadership also offers formal training opportunities and incentives for acquiring that knowledge. In addition, Starbucks executives understand something that few business leaders do: sharing knowledge with customers makes for more sophisticated consumers. As a result, these customers develop a passion for your products and services and are eager to explore the subtle nuances of what your business offers.

Today, in what has been aptly called a knowledge and service economy, each of us adds value to our business by enhancing the customer's experience. In return, customers offer our business their loyalty and come to see us as trusted advisors rather than just transaction handlers.

Formal Training

At Starbucks, all partners are encouraged to develop a knowledge of coffee that can lead to personal insights for customers. For example, partners use their knowledge to help customers appreciate how fresh, high-quality coffee provides a rich taste profile through the aromatic gases that the coffee releases. This knowledge acquisition is fostered by the leadership through initiatives such as the "coffee passport" program, where new partners are given a 104-page booklet that they complete within their first 90 days of employment.

The booklet includes a map of coffee-growing regions, information on coffee farming and roasting, coffee-tasting terms, the fundamentals of brewing coffee, a complementary flavors chart, and a list of Starbucks coffee offerings. Partners are expected to not only use the passport as a reference, but complete verified tastings of all Starbucks core coffees twice a year. Additionally, Starbucks partners are given a pound of coffee each week at no charge to ensure that they are continuing to develop their knowledge of and refined taste for Starbucks products.

As they develop, baristas are encouraged to explore the possibility of becoming "Coffee Masters," a designation reserved for Starbucks partners who have a passion to become true coffee experts. To achieve that designation and don a black apron, a barista must complete a significant number of hours of paid training, pass a series of content-based tests with high proficiency, and lead a number of coffee tastings.

Normally, this training occurs over a period of about three months and involves presenting seminars and topical sessions. While it makes sense for customer-facing partners like baristas to get this education, Starbucks leadership is encouraging this certification throughout the organization. As a result, it is not unusual to see Coffee Master seminars being given in the marketing and legal departments—or just about any other department or area within the Starbucks organization, including support staff.

Training is an expensive proposition, and therefore it is usually one of the first budget items that gets cut when a company needs to boost its bottom line. In light of that reality, one might wonder why Starbucks spends so much on training, even though it is almost impossible to measure the actual financial impact of that training.

The answer lies in the adage "Knowledge is power." The more an employee knows about a product—its origins, its properties—the greater the difference that employee can make in a customer's life. No matter what the product or

Create Your Own Experience

- How is your organization ensuring that all staff members take advantage of their opportunity to improve the company by improving their core competencies and advanced information base?

- How committed are you to sharing your knowledge in order to generate passion and awareness in your colleagues and customers?

- How can you add value to yourself and your organization?

service, customers rely on knowledgeable people to help them, and they remember those people and businesses when they have additional needs. While difficult to measure, the power of knowledge makes training a well-placed investment for Starbucks and its customers.

Be Involved

From the perspective of Starbucks leadership, *being involved* means active participation "in the store, in the company, and in the community." In today's lightning-paced world, businesses have dismal futures when their employees try to get away with doing the bare minimum. Successful businesses thrive on the sweat and tears of colleagues who know how to grasp the right opportunities. Leaders encourage employees to go beyond just doing their day-to-day job, and instead invest attentive, creative, and passionate energy.

By being attentive, front-line partners observe the evolving wants and needs of the customers. This, in turn, encourages a "yes, I will" attitude—where breakthrough products and service are created. Sadly, many people are either afraid or unwilling to fully immerse themselves in the possibilities that surround them at work—or, for that matter, in life. They do what is expected, and that's all.

The leadership of a business can also suffer from a "do the minimum" mentality. Some view the company as an island unto itself, separate from the community and society as a whole. Starbucks and many other businesses understand that an organization, no matter how large or how small, can become an asset to the community it serves.

Starbucks leaders capture the passion and vitality of their people by encouraging the 100,000-plus partners to take an

37

active role at the store, business, and community levels. Howard Schultz sees the link between involvement and entrepreneurship by noting in an interview with *Know*™, "People want to be part of something bigger than themselves. They want to be part of something that touches their hearts."

Involvement in the Store

One of the best ways to become involved is to look around your office or store—much like a crime scene investigator—for clues on how to make the customer experiences and the business better. One group of baristas at a California Starbucks did this and noticed that there were a significant number of deaf customers visiting regularly. The baristas then elected to take signing lessons on their own time to communicate with those customers more effectively.

As a result of these efforts, Starbucks reputation in the deaf community spread well beyond that California location. In fact, Starbucks is now a prominent meeting location for deaf patrons in the United States and Canada and is cited on www.deafcoffee.com, an Internet site with information on how to join or start a coffee club for deaf patrons. These clubs serve deaf customers who want to meet, chat, and drink coffee together at Starbucks and other supportive meeting areas.

In-Store Improvements

Because management encourages Starbucks partners to be involved in the company, partners often look at how they can improve the manner in which customer needs are served. Partner Rick Mace, who worked at the original Starbucks store in Seattle, reported that the staff members noticed they were having problems processing customer orders after the Pike Place Market store was renovated.

Rick suggested that when the store was redesigned, "it created a change in the flow, and there were so many people in this store that you couldn't hear when the register partners called the drink orders to the bar. Between the register partner's mouth and the barista's ear at the bar were two espresso grinders that were constantly humming and whirring. So the partners got together and developed a system where they could get the cups already marked at the registers and then advance them to the bar."

By being open to innovation, the team came up with a very successful system that not only allowed better customer service, but also made the workplace more fun for the partners. Rick explains, "Rather than walking about 25 or 26 feet down to the end of a counter, partners decided to throw the cups with the customer's name and drink noted on them from the register to the espresso bar."

This simple change not only evoked a spirit of fun, increased the speed of service, and created an engaging visual, but also tied in nicely with the antics of a neighboring business, the Pike Place Fish Market, which was famed for its employees throwing fish from the fish display to the register.

39

Involvement in the Business

Starbucks management makes a point of listening and responding to the ideas and suggestions of partners. The result of this interest is that partners frequently take responsibility for suggesting and championing new product ideas based on the input they get from customers. By involving themselves in product development and expansion of services, partners take a proactive approach to the future of the business. Rather than waiting for cues from the home office, everyone at Starbucks is charged with searching for new and better ideas for meeting and exceeding customer needs.

This phenomenon of partners suggesting innovative Starbucks products occurs in all parts of the globe. Dai Ichikawa, team manager for Beverages and Whole Bean in Tokyo, Japan, tells of a former store manager (and current Coffee Heritage team manager), Hiromitsu Hatta, who wondered if "jelly cubes," a popular dessert in that country, could be added to a Frappuccino® blended beverage. Dai says, "I was a district manager at the time when Hiromitsu was playing around with a coffee gelatin product in the back room of his store. He showed it to me, and we decided to try it the next summer. It was a success, and we rolled it out throughout Japan."

When Coffee Jelly Frappuccino® blended beverage made its appearance in all of Japan's Starbucks, it was labor-intensive. As Dai indicates, "Initially we made the jelly cubes in the store. We brewed the coffee, cut the coffee jelly into cubes, and added it to the bottom of a Coffee Frappuccino® blended beverage. As time went on, we found an easier way to make this summer treat." It required a lot of work for Hiromitsu to go to a local store, buy gelatin, and play with formulas in his Starbucks store. But as Hiromitsu simply explains, "It was the right thing to do. This is my company."

Additionally, when asked why he decided to share his idea with his district manager, Hiromitsu noted, "Because I knew he would listen and determine it was good for our customers." Leadership has created the expectation that partners are to be involved in improving Starbucks and has gone the extra step of creating a culture in which partners expect to be heard when they offer ideas.

Most business advances simply come from a persistent focus on ways to make the customer's life easier. Dina Campion, a Los Angeles district manager (who is credited in part with the creation of Starbucks Frappuccino® blended beverage), highlights drive-throughs in the category of customer convenience: "At Starbucks, these came about absolutely from our people listening to the desire of customers. People, particularly women, kept telling our baristas that it would be nice if they could drive through and get their coffee. In my area we have a higher percentage of women in our customer base; many of the people we serve are between their mid-twenties and their late thirties. A lot of those women have children. Getting out of your car with two kids in a car seat to run in and get a cup of coffee can become a chore. Ultimately, by listening to our customers, we recognized the convenience of drive-throughs, and in turn that listening has had a huge impact on the business."

Be Involved in the Community

Community involvement can take many forms, from creating a community meeting place, to supporting community events, to staff volunteering in community-related activities. Starbucks leadership encourages and supports engagement in all of these areas. Starbucks store manager Nerieda Hernandez shares a simple way in which Starbucks partners offered their talents and their business's space to the community.

"We had an open-mike night," explains Nerieda. "Some of our partners performed, and community members performed. It started out small as we posted a bulletin board inside our store. It became a huge event. The open-mike night was so successful that customers were requesting it more often than once a month. It was diverse and great fun for all ages. Of course, we'd offer food and beverage samples."

Other Starbucks partners find and address community-based needs through their stores. This brings with it heartfelt appreciation from the community. Robin Jones, who worked in a technology training center in Columbus, Ohio, saw the positive impact of the Starbucks partners on a group of people with whom she was involved.

As Robin reflects, "We offered free training to the unemployed and underemployed members of the community. Because we were located in the heart of downtown, many of our students were homeless. Many of them had had nothing to eat prior to coming to class. Some would come and stay all day, just to get the food Starbucks partners donated."

Lauren Moore, director of Community Relations and Giving, shares, "What we bring is the power of our people and our product and our brand to make a significant impact. And so the programs that we're looking for with our people are ones where they have volunteer opportunities; they can get actively involved."

Create Your Own Experience

- Who can benefit from the opportunity to partner with you for the good of the community or for mutual business benefits?

- What opportunities have you missed in your workplace?

- Where can you dive in with your passion and involvement?

It doesn't matter what your business is; people want to make a difference. When leaders encourage involvement and the sharing of ideas that affect both the business and the community, the staff is given opportunities to be more engaged and effective.

Make It Your Own: Five Ways of Being as a Legacy

The Five Ways of Being and the *Green Apron Book* reflect the core values of Starbucks. In many companies, these values would only be hanging on a plaque at the corporate office. At Starbucks, however, they come to life. They have been fully embraced by the leadership team and are well integrated into the Starbucks culture. Starbucks management understands the importance of leading by example. This can be seen in the very top leadership of the company.

At a retirement party for Orin Smith, outgoing president and CEO, held at the Starbucks Support Center, Jim Donald, his replacement, spoke of Orin: "If you look at all the attributes: be genuine, be welcoming, be considerate, be knowledgeable, be involved . . . that really *is* Orin Smith, in every way, in every corner, in every country in which we operate. The biggest thing we can do for Orin is to continue to build on his legacy, to make sure that the Five Ways of Being are alive and well in this building, and that they're alive and well as you go out into stores—whether it's your neighborhood, it's in the United States, Canada, or any other country where we operate. That's the biggest tribute that we can give Orin. We must continue to ramp this up."

Starbucks leadership does ramp up the Make It Your Own concept at all levels of the organization. This concept is infused into the Starbucks Experience and into employee empowerment as well. Others have already taken notice of the power of the Starbucks Five Ways of Being. Dr. Theresa (Terri) Stahlman, regional superintendent of the Duval County Public Schools, in Jacksonville, Florida, notes, "We basically took the *Green Apron Book* and aligned it exactly with what we do in the business of education. The Starbucks Ways of Being are great tools for helping our school leaders frame ways to be more effective with all they serve."

They have Made It Their Own at Starbucks and in the Duval County School District. Now, how can the Five Ways of Being work in your company?

Ideas to Sip On

Companies benefit when all employees understand business priorities and look for ways to bring their individual creativity and passion to meet those objectives.

- By being welcoming, Starbucks forges a bond that invites customers back to visit again and again.

- To be genuine means to connect, discover, and respond.

- Listening is just one part of creating a connection with customers. Businesses also need to discover each customer's needs and unique situation and then find ways to meet those needs.

- Being considerate is less about being polite and more about being mindful of the needs of others while creating win/win situations. It should empower you to act in ways that consider the needs of others.

- Be knowledgeable, love what you do, and share your knowledge with others.

- In a knowledge and service economy, we add value to a business by enhancing the customer's experience.

- Be involved—in your store or office, in the company at large, and in your community.

everything matters

*"Too often we underestimate the power of
a touch, a smile, a kind word, a listening ear,
an honest compliment, or the smallest act
of caring, all of which have the potential
to turn a life around."*

—LEO BUSCAGLIA

Howard Schultz is fond of saying that "retail is detail." In reality—although this lacks the rhyming charm of Howard's quote—*all* business is detail. When details are overlooked or missed, even the most patient of customers can be frustrated, and costly errors can occur. Unfortunately, only a small percentage of unhappy customers bring their complaints directly to management. They simply go elsewhere, spending their hard-earned dollars at competitors' stores and sharing their grievances with scores of family members, friends, and acquaintances.

Starbucks leaders understand that their successful ship can go down if they fail to take care of both the "below-deck" (unseen aspects) and "above-deck" (customer-facing) components of the customer experience. As unfair as it may seem, in the world of business Everything Matters. The moment you think something doesn't matter . . . be ready to start bailing.

Attention to Detail Occurs by Design, Not by Default

Starbucks success, in part, is linked to the amazing ability of partners to zero in on the minute details that matter greatly to customers. In a nutshell, Starbucks leadership appreciates diverse concerns such as the importance of the physical environment, the quality of the product, the need to set priorities for the workforce, the importance of the company's reputation in the larger world, and even the playfulness of the culture. A great cup of coffee is only part of the Starbucks success equation.

Jim Donald, Starbucks president and CEO, put it well when he suggested, "We can't let the coffee down. Day in and day out, we have to consistently execute on the details." That execution requires diligent attention to everything that goes into the customer's visit. Much of that focus can be found in the physical environment that sets the stage for the Starbucks Experience. For this reason, every aspect of the business that touches the coffee—creating a third place, ensuring the highest level of product quality, excelling at customer service, and building a rewarding culture—must reflect the highest standards possible.

Everything Matters: Creating an Environment for the Starbucks Experience

Starbucks management understands that a competitive advantage occurs when everyone in a company appreciates that nothing is trivial and that customers notice everything. As a result, Starbucks leaders have taken great pains to execute their strategy precisely—right down to the last coffee bean. Perhaps as important, leadership has worked tirelessly to perfect every aspect of the store design, making sure to balance functionality with a warm and friendly ambience.

As an article by the Corporate Design Foundation, a nonprofit education and research organization dedicated to improving the effectiveness of businesses, states,

The Starbucks sensation is driven not just by the quality of its products but by the entire atmosphere surrounding the purchase of coffee: the openness of its store space, . . . interesting menu boards, the shape of its counter, . . . the cleanliness of the floorboards. . . . What Starbucks recognized long before its imitators was that the art of retailing coffee went way beyond prod-

49

*uct. The details of the total experience mattered. . . .
Every particular—from napkins to coffee bags, store-
fronts to window seats, annual reports to mail order cat-
alogs, tabletops to thermal carafes—seems to reflect . . .
the authentic and organic roots of Starbucks.*

Top management at Starbucks appreciated from the outset that the atmosphere of the company's shops would be a
key driver of success. Starting in 1991, Starbucks assembled
an in-house group of architects and designers to work to
ensure that each store would convey a consistent image and
character. At the same time, these designers were encouraged
to experiment with a broad range of store formats, from flag-
ship stores in brisk traffic areas and highly visible locations
to kiosks in supermarkets and building lobbies. To take
design up yet another level, Starbucks assembled a "stores of
the future" project team to create a vision of the next gener-
ation of Starbucks stores. Starbucks leadership not only
focuses on today's details, but strives to anticipate the detailed
needs of the future.

Members of the design team have been required to start
their careers at Starbucks by working behind the counters.
Knowing how store design interfaces with the needs of customers and baristas allows these partners to develop work-
spaces that are both aesthetic and functional. Few Fortune
500 companies go to such lengths to make sure that key
visionaries and planners are so in touch with the needs of customers. When such an effort occurs, it pays off both for the
business and for its customers. For example, in the French
Les Capucines store, design team members decided to invest
in preserving an elegant nineteenth-century ceiling with its
painted frescoes, gold beading, crystal chandeliers, and mar-

ble pillars. Although the ceiling was not protected by local planning codes, Starbucks leadership understood the importance of incorporating that unique, historic charm into its Parisian Starbucks Experience.

In order to maintain this special connection with customers, leadership at Starbucks is continuously searching for new ways to improve all aspects of the store environment. Starbucks started playing music in its stores simply to set a comfortable atmosphere. The former store manager and current programming manager in Starbucks Hear Music division, Timothy Jones, was encouraged to take music to a higher level. Rather than simply being in the background, music emerged as an important detail in creating a truly unique Starbucks Experience.

Timothy, who had previously owned a record store, was given the latitude to use his music background to actively explore ways to enhance the customers' time in a Starbucks store. Timothy enthusiastically explained: "With the blessing of management, I started programming the playlists for our in-store music. The idea was that customized selections could provide a unique, warm, consistent enrichment to the customer experience. I think leadership realized that people come in for coffee, but we can give them more while they're there. If we can entertain them and send them out with an idea, a tool, something to discover, then we're a bigger stop than just a cup of coffee." That is the essence of great business leadership—finding ways to deliver existing products and services in ways that make the brand more significant to the customer. In Timothy's words, we must make the experience "a bigger stop."

To create this bigger stop, Timothy explains how Starbucks managers start with an unwavering commitment to the

51

details of the customer experience. As it relates to packaging Starbucks music offerings, he suggests, "We care about the little things. When we decided to give customers a chance to bring Starbucks music home by selling compilation CDs, we packaged the CDs in digi-packs. A digi-pack is where a CD is wrapped in attractive cardboard rather than in a jewel case to give the CD a soft feel. We made sure that there was a lot of artwork and that the offering was beautiful. Digis fit with Starbucks; the jewel case just didn't feel like us. The cardboard, the recycled paper—that was Starbucks."

Details matter, right down to the choice of the materials that wrap CDs. Not only must the details be right, but the *blending* of those details must be carefully crafted to make sure that every aspect of the experience comes together to create the Starbucks identity.

The Starbucks brand is more than just an appealing presentation of goods. New products must be offered for sale in a way that fits with what customers have come to know and expect from the company. As Timothy explains, "We don't want our partners doing suggestive selling of the music, since that is more likely to annoy customers than please them. We don't want to hear, 'Would you like to get one of our CDs today with that latte?' That's not the third place, that's not the coffeehouse, that's not the Starbucks Experience. Yes, we have merchandise, but it needs to fit into the environment. The Dean Martin CD needs to be inviting, but consistent with the rest of the customer experience, and it's all the better if you see it while 'That's Amore' plays overhead."

Managers have to constantly put themselves in the shoes of their customers, seeing everything from the other side of the counter. This perspective has helped make Starbucks the valued brand it is today. Through leadership's vigilance, details come together to make an indelible mark on the millions who enter Starbucks stores every day. These leaders know that even if they have executed consistently for a significant period of time, they will ultimately be judged on their ability to bring the details together now and in the future. Small missteps often dramatically tarnish great brands.

While the first principle in the Starbucks Experience looks at the way partners are encouraged to "be," the Everything Matters principle reflects the importance of solid processes and procedures in daily operations. This operational focus ensures consistency for customer visits across Starbucks stores.

Creating the ideal environment depends on disciplined quality control safeguards that give structure to the customer experience. Barista Meredith Kotas explains how Starbucks guarantees that customers receive consistent quality from store to store: "We have a basic line of deployment that we all understand, where person A is on the register, person B stays on the bar, and person C is floating around making drinks if there's a long line. That's standard at every Starbucks store. We also have checklists. They include all the things that just have to happen, like cleaning the counters, making sure all the prep is stocked, sanitizing the tongs, and making sure the pastry plates are always clean. My manager has instilled the importance of this into us, and we don't have to even look at the list. Our brewed coffees, in theory, would be good for about five hours in the container in which they're made. But we brew a new container every hour to ensure that they're very fresh, very hot. It's the freshest coffee you'll get."

If you think customers don't pay attention when a detail is out of alignment, think again. In support of this point, Meredith relates a specific customer's reaction: "One time a barista wasn't paying attention to the timer. He had failed to

53

brew coffee within the hour and served a cup that had been brewed an hour and 10 minutes earlier. The customer, who was a regular, immediately noticed a difference. People who are real coffee connoisseurs appreciate our focus on the little things." Commitment to detail is critical in all businesses. If you ignore the smaller things that are important to those you serve, you'll fail to create the experience they crave. This inattention will be a surefire way to drive those customers straight to your competitors.

Starbucks leadership has found that implementing strict quality control measures frees partners to look for new ways to deliver extraordinary experiences. Meredith shares: "I particularly like the requirement that one of the store partners

Create Your Own Experience

- How do you and your business attend to the details that affect the experience you wish to create?

- Where can you execute more consistently on details, so that people will talk about being a shareholder in your company?

- When has your customer experience been compromised by missed details, even when the product you received was a quality one?

- What can you do to put yourself more directly into the experience of your customer?

- What quality control safeguards can you employ to assist your team in attending to important details that are frequently missed?

check the café every 10 minutes. It gives us a chance to get out from behind the counter to make sure everything is clean and orderly, and we become more involved with our customers. I was doing this when a customer dropped a doppio espresso. I picked it up and said, 'Let me make you a new one.' He responded, 'No need to bother. I was almost done.' I commented, 'It's not a bother, so I'm going to make you a fresh beverage on the house.' As I came back with his replacement drink, the man was amazed. Then he said, 'It's behavior like this that caused me to buy Starbucks stock.'" At Starbucks, the Everything Matters approach not only results in powerful emotional connections with customers, but even encourages customers to share in the success of the business.

Details Converge into a "Felt Sense" about the Business

55

Often we can't specifically describe what causes us to feel a certain way, but we know our "global emotional reaction." Psychologist Dr. Eugene Gendlin coined the term *felt sense* in his best-selling book *Experiencing and the Creation of Meaning* to describe these general emotional responses. A felt sense ultimately is the result of a myriad of tiny details that lurk somewhere below our conscious awareness. For example, without conjuring up specifics, the term *ice cream* is likely to bring about a very different felt sense from the word *vinegar*.

When it comes to Starbucks, large and diverse groups of people—partners and customers alike—often have a common and shared felt sense about the brand and the stores. Consistently, people experience Starbucks as warm, comfortable, and pleasurable. Most of these individuals probably don't spend a lot of time thinking about what contributes to their "gut reaction," but others clearly track the details that generate their positive emotional responses.

A barista from Columbus, Ohio, puts it this way: "We pay attention to that atmosphere. We are vigilant about the music in the background, pleasant colors, comfortable furniture, and the right amount of lighting. I make sure the tables are clean and the carpet is not littered with crumbs, except for major eating incidents here and there, mostly involving children and pastries. I do my part to keep it warm and inviting. I want my Starbucks store to be open and airy for our customers. I want the details to reach out and say 'Come in and stay awhile.'"

Customers value the detailed attention given to a business's ambience. For customer Beth Jones, Starbucks produces a felt sense that is almost like a minivacation. "One of the things I love most about Starbucks is the relaxed atmosphere. Nobody tells you to leave or gives you a dirty look if you've been there over a half hour, unlike a certain donut haven I know. It's a great place to go to talk with that special someone, catch up with an old friend, or escape after a stressful day at work. You can't go to Disney World every day, unfortunately, so Starbucks is my affordable luxury."

Whether it is this sense of affordable luxury or some other emotional response, the individuality of customers draws them to specific aspects of a business's environment. Customer Leslie Alter reports that she particularly enjoys the way Starbucks offers her a positive change in atmosphere. "It's not quiet at Starbucks, and that's why I come here. If I wanted quiet, I'd sit in my apartment. I like the music, and I like the noise, and I like the atmosphere—the people talking, the pumping of the machines, the choice of songs they play. I even notice subtle differences between stores."

Those differences that Leslie is referring to reflect a choice made by Starbucks leadership to consciously meld consistent environmental features in its store designs with community-based nuances. As noted in the book *Strategic Management: Concepts and Cases,*

> *Starbucks management looked upon each store as a billboard for the company and as a contributor to building the company's brand and image. Each detail was scrutinized to enhance the mood and ambience of the store, to make sure everything signaled "best of class" and that it reflected the personality of the community and the neighborhood. The thesis was "Everything matters." The company went to great lengths to make sure the store fixtures, the merchandise displays, the colors, the artwork, the banners, the music, and the aromas all blended to create a consistent, inviting, stimulating environment that evoked the romance of coffee, that signaled the company's passion for coffee, and that rewarded customers with ceremony, stories, and surprise. Starbucks was recognized for its sensitivity to neighborhood conservation with the Scenic America's award for excellent design and "sensitive reuse of spaces within cities."*

Just to show the importance of the environment, customer Devin Page suggests, "Starbucks could very well operate without even selling coffee. They could charge an entrance fee and offer nothing else but a room and mellow Bob Marley music softly playing in the background, and people would still come. Starbucks recognizes the niche they fill." Even when customers don't consciously track the details, those details—whether managed well or overlooked—often result

57

in the lingering impression that customers have of a company. Great leaders look for ways to maximize the felt sense that their business generates. In order to do this, these leaders help their people execute on the minute but significant details that positively affect the way they are viewed.

Never Cut Corners on Quality

From the perspective of Starbucks management, few things affect the reputation of a business more than a resounding Everything Matters approach to quality. While managers in some businesses think that they can cut corners without compromising their company's brand or reputation, particularly in unseen (below-deck) areas, they are mistaken.

To put it simply, the vast majority of shortcuts backfire. This is illustrated by the story of a wealthy man who asked a builder to spare no expense in creating his mansion. Since the man was out of the country while the home was being constructed, the builder decided that he could make the infrastructure out of inferior material and cover it up with superior finish work. The builder could then overcharge the man based on the home's appearance. When the owner returned to the country, he was so taken by the beauty of the home that he told the builder, "This is simply too nice a house for me. Here, you take the keys."

There is no hidden inferior material at Starbucks. On the contrary, Starbucks epitomizes a company that has achieved amazing success by not compromising on quality. Management at Starbucks takes pride in the quality of the products the company serves, instilling a passion for excellence by centrally placing the demand for quality in the company's mission statement. That statement asserts that Starbucks partners

will "apply the highest standards of excellence to the purchasing, roasting and fresh delivery of our coffee."
To that end, Starbucks leaders do what is necessary to meet or exceed their quality standards, even when this means abandoning the "old way" of doing things. The leaders are constantly researching and developing technologies and systems to improve the consistency of the company's roasting process and the freshness of the coffee. This commitment to innovation in the service of product quality has had a significant impact on the ability of Starbucks coffee to reach a broader customer base and expand into national and international markets.

Many of these innovations have been achieved by dedicated partners at the Starbucks roasting plant in Kent, Washington. Tom Walters, the communications coordinator of this original roasting plant, says, "Since I started here in 1982, freshness is all Starbucks has done. We were selling specialty coffee back at a time when specialty coffee had a 1 percent market share. More people owned airplanes than espresso machines. Until 1987, wholesale coffee went out to restaurants in five-pound paper lunch bags and had a seven-day shelf life. Starbucks was a pretty small company. My job was to drive the 1968 Ford Econoline van and deliver the paper bags to restaurants in downtown Seattle. When I did my deliveries, I went through their coffee. It was in our contract with the restaurants that any coffee over seven days old would be taken back by us, and we'd receive no reimbursement. Starbucks wanted to keep restaurants from serving our coffee when it was stale." Tom adds that if it hadn't been for a commitment to quality and attention to the "little things," Starbucks would never have made it out of Seattle.

Not only did Starbucks leadership demonstrate an unconventional preoccupation with quality, but it was willing to pay the financial price for that commitment. From the stand-point of product excellence, Tom, who has worked as a roaster in the Kent plant, shares, "What defines coffee as fresh is that it actively gives off 3 to 20 times its volume in aromatic gas. It was expensive for us to keep those aromatic gases available until the coffee was brewed. In order to do so, 10 percent of our product was returned to our plant."

While many companies would have balked at that return rate and decided to throw in the towel, Starbucks knew that there had to be a better way to secure freshness. "The company and its collective quality and manufacturing teams worked to develop packaging that enabled us to keep the coffee fresh, not for seven days, but for up to six weeks," continues Tom, "and that let us expand throughout the Northwest. Starbucks leadership would never have tried that expansion if the coffee could not get to its location and be ground and brewed fresh."

Thanks to this passion for quality and commitment to innovation, Starbucks management was able to reduce the amount of coffee the company scrapped and ultimately made sure Starbucks coffee could be delivered fresh anywhere in the world. At times, Starbucks leaders had to push suppliers of their packaging material to go beyond current technology. This led to innovations in the small things like improved packaging materials and a 7-cent valve that lets gases out of the bag but does not allow air to enter, which would make the coffee stale.

Rich Soderberg, senior vice president of Manufacturing, notes, "This journey from seven days of freshness took us many years and numerous innovations. We had to sever relationships with suppliers who were unable to innovate in a way that delivered the freshness we demanded. Each step of the way we needed to know that we would have the freshest coffee in the market." This detailed focus on innovation was painstaking. Rich suggests, "It happened through very planned and very conservative methodologies, and above all, it required our partners' dedication to making sure that our packages were made right at the factory and that our quality control people secured the freshness we needed. We could never have become the company we are today if our coffee had only a seven-day shelf life." From Rich's perspective, "Our success in part begins with a willingness to challenge conventional thinking while paying attention to details that allow us to innovate. This approach offers the competitive advantage that we enjoy."

Details matter, from 7-cent valves to passionate and innovative partners at the manufacturing level. By focusing on quality, innovation, and the smallest aspects of business, Starbucks is an example of how an enduring brand emerges, not only through management at the macro level (strategic), but through management at the micro level (operational) as well. While great leaders spend most of their time looking at big-picture, strategic opportunities, they cannot overlook the systems and training necessary to ensure the quality of every aspect of the company's products, services, and processes.

Sometimes details need to be managed well beyond the confines of the business itself. Long before customers take their first sip of Breakfast Blend at their neighborhood Starbucks, the staff in the Starbucks Coffee Department has gone to great lengths behind the scenes, looking for and developing quality coffee in the various countries of origin. Coffee quality begins with the relationships that Starbucks partners forge with coffee farmers so that the growers bring the highest-quality coffee to Starbucks coffee purchasers. Without high-grade coffee beans, Starbucks is incapable of bringing high-quality coffee to the cups of its customers. According to Dub Hay, senior vice president of Coffee and Global Procurement,

> It is a very detailed process that we consistently go through. When we go to origin countries, we don't buy coffee on farms. When we go to farms, we are there to look at their trees. We may taste coffee at the farm, but we never buy it there; we only buy it once we are able to take coffee back into conditions that we can control, and that are always the same. We can examine it, sample it, resample it, and compare it with other coffees we think are interesting.

In addition to the coffee itself, many seemingly unrelated details are considered, all of which contribute to the coffee's current and future quality. It is not enough for experts in the Coffee Department to find a great-tasting coffee at a specific farm. They have to know that high-quality coffee will be available from that farm well into the future and that the business practices of the supplier will fit with Starbucks values. While many business leaders may convince themselves that they are not responsible for the actions of their suppliers, Starbucks leadership sees this distinction as very shortsighted.

As Dub explains, "The quality of the coffee is not enough. We want to know about the quality of the people with whom we do business. We want to know about their integrity and their commitment to future excellence. To that end, we look for the health of the farms. We pay attention to how the farmers treat the environment. We look at how they treat the social conditions on the farm. What's the altitude? What's the variety? Is it shade grown? What's the yield per hectare (a unit of measurement equivalent to approximately two and one-half acres)? What are the farmers like? Are there buffer zones between fields and streams? Is there is a mill there? What are they doing with the wastewater? How much water are they generating that needs to be processed? Does the coffee move through, or are there hang-ups that can create problems with quality? We want to know how transparent people are in terms of sharing money all the way down to the coffee picker. All of this is considered before we buy our crop, because anyone can buy coffee; it is *how* we buy coffee that makes Starbucks special."

For Dub Hay and other Starbucks leaders, quality lives not only in the coffee they can buy today, but in the relationships they forge for the future. It is through these relationships that Starbucks can work with farmers to continually improve product quality. Rather than making impulsive business decisions that address only short-term business needs, Starbucks leadership is willing to forgo stopgap measures in favor of longer-term relationship-based solutions.

In essence, the Starbucks management approach teaches that quality business relationships are essential to long-term growth and survival. Being vigilant and careful about those with whom you associate ultimately protects your business and your brand. Looking into the details of how potential business partners conduct themselves safeguards you against developing relationships that will fail in the future. Starbucks coffee buyers say "no" to coffee farmers who don't fit with the values and quality priorities that Starbucks demands over the long term. While some relationship details can be overlooked in the short term, stockholders, partners, and future generations of customers will be adversely affected if sus-

63

tainability, social factors, and enduring strategic partnership arrangements are not properly addressed up front.

Prioritizing Objectives and Keeping Them in Front of Your People

While the details discussed thus far—environmental factors and product quality—may be on the radar screens of many business leaders, other critical business issues are frequently overlooked. As suggested in Principle 1 in the discussion of the importance of being knowledgeable, training programs are often expendable. When the economy turns bad or business hits a rough patch, training and education budgets suffer. This short-term financial fix often compromises the long-term health of the company. For Starbucks leadership, however, educational programs are a critical detail in the future of the business.

Starbucks management is constantly enhancing and perfecting training resources, not only at the product knowledge and operational levels, but also in areas that help partners take ownership in the business. When it comes to keeping the Principle 1, "Make It Your Own," behaviors alive and dynamic, shift supervisors, store managers, and other managers participate in a process called *exploring customer stories*. At the store level, partners are offered excerpts taken from real customer comments and are then asked to identify behaviors from the *Green Apron Book* that they would choose if they were in that situation.

A partner might receive the following customer statement: "My wife and I decided to buy a Starbucks Card ($50) for our good friend as a birthday gift last week. When we arrived in your store, I carefully told the cashier that I needed to purchase a card with $50 for our friend. Because she was joking with others and did not pay attention to our request, she added only $15 on the card without confirming it with us. . . . Twenty minutes later we gave the card to our friend and told him that there was $50 on it. You can imagine how embarrassed we were when our friend finally told us that there was only $15 on the card. Therefore, we went back to the store to reload the $35 on the card for my friend. It wasted our time to take care of it, and we were upset."

Managers are then asked to reflect on the customer's experience, with questions such as

- Name three behaviors that detracted from legendary service.

- What *Green Apron Book* behaviors could have made this situation a positive experience for the customer?

- How would you coach the partner in this situation?

Rather than responding to hypothetical customer experiences, managers are given the opportunity to anticipate situations that their staff will encounter, based on positive and negative real-world customer transactions. The training also reinforces for management the corporate priorities outlined in the Five Ways of Being. In addition, this approach helps leaders teach their partners by encouraging them to coach their teams to greater competence in delivering legendary service.

Similarly, Starbucks partners, at the barista level, have access to something called *Conversations and Connections,* a tool used to facilitate discussion and regular storytelling about behaviors, actions, and language consistent with the Five Ways of Being. *Conversations and Connections* is provided so that in-store partners can read, analyze, and discuss customer stories. It gives partners additional opportunities to relate actual situations to the behaviors and actions encouraged in the *Green Apron Book.*

Each week, *Conversations and Connections* centers on a particular Way of Being. On a *be knowledgeable* theme week, the following customer story was provided:

> *I just wanted to thank Ashley for being so kind and helpful. I had a question about one of your beverages and she took the time and care to explain the product and then took time to create a sample. I really appreciate her thoughtfulness.*
>
> Store #76304, Target #1834, Pomona, CA

After reading the example, partners are given a quick review of how Ashley made a difference for the comment writer:

- She learned how to describe coffee. This customer said Ashley was able to explain the product that she had a question about.

- She shared her coffee knowledge, passion, and excitement through a tasting and made a sample of the product she was describing for the customer.

These brief examples help partners identify with the customer experience and reinforce the guiding principles that are most valued in the Starbucks culture. According to Jennifer Ames-Karreman, director of Customer Service Operations/Customer Care Manager, the *Conversations and Connections* tool has a variety of benefits for Starbucks. "When we ask new partners about this approach, they tell us it helped them rapidly become a part of their team. They feel confident more quickly because they can anticipate customer experiences and learn from positive and negative scenarios. They experience accelerated learning. More seasoned partners feel the scenarios acknowledge their efforts with customers. They appreciate that the company as a whole is giving attention to what they do by sharing their stories. When a positive story is presented, we list the store number at the bottom so everybody knows who did something right. The stories then serve as a form of recognition as well."

Ultimately, any business leader can look for ways to use customer or client feedback as a learning tool. Such training not only shows employees how to excel at their jobs, but also motivates them, keeps them engaged, and builds team spirit.

Starbucks managers have seen benefits from other training initiatives as well. In addition to providing straightforward customer feedback to partners, Starbucks leaders create playful ways to emphasize problem solving consistent with the Five Ways of Being. Specifically, they have developed a training game called *Starbucks Experience from the Inside Out*. The goal of the game is to secure a human connection with the customer. To do this, the partner tries to understand more than just the customer's external presentation and attempts to understand the customer's internal experience.

The game uses dice, game cards, and a game tablet and starts with a role-playing exercise between two partners, one who plays the barista and another who plays the customer. In the game, the designated customer reads context information that is written on the outside of a game card. It may say something like, "I'm shopping for whole bean coffee, and I stop and smile at the barista." Then the "customer" rolls the dice to determine what's happening in the store, how many people are in line, the time of day, and other factors that

67

set the stage for everyone to appreciate what's happening in the scenario.

Before the interaction between the person playing the customer and the person playing the partner begins, the customer alone reads the inside of the card, which explains the internal experience she is to act out. The customer may use body language or words to communicate her internal experience, but she cannot actually say what she is feeling. The partner attempts to handle the situation empathetically and gets feedback from the customer, and from observers, on how well he connected with the *Green Apron* behaviors. At this point, the designated customer reveals what was actually happening on the inside, for her.

In the game, each round is "won" if the customer feels that the partner connected with what was most important to her at the time of her visit and if a memorable experience was created. An example of a game card is as follows:

Visual cues from the customer
You are humming holiday tunes
and seem to be cheerful, but are visibly in a hurry.

What is going on for the customer on the inside?
You couldn't resist stopping for a beverage, but you only have 20 minutes before you're supposed to be back to work for the holiday potluck. You haven't picked anything up yet for the party and still have to stop at the grocery store.

When this game was introduced as a training tool, Starbucks leadership presented it strategically, one group at a time. Jennifer Ames-Karreman explains, "We first debuted the game for management teams. They played it by picking somebody to be the partner and somebody to be the customer. Other managers served as observers. The game has become popular among many of those managers, and some are finding new ways to make it applicable in broader training settings."

Clearly, Starbucks philosophy is that training doesn't need to be boring, conventional, or mundane. In addition to playing the game with in-store partners, Starbucks leadership has added a twist to the game by having managers not only watch the interaction in the role play, but then solicit feedback from the person role-playing the customer. The manager then uses that customer feedback in a coaching session with the partner who offered the service. This allows the manager to rehearse ways to most effectively transfer the subjective experience of the customer into constructive training for the partner. In a playful way, the game offers training opportunities that challenge baristas and managers to anticipate customer situations, demonstrate sensitivity, use sound judgment, and enhance their problem-solving abilities. The results are amazing, as playful means lead to such important ends.

69

Creating a Playful Corporate Culture

Board games for training! That's just another example of how everything matters in a dynamic corporate culture. Starbucks leadership understands that playful and positive work environments produce vital and engaged staff members. Regional director Carla Archambault shares the importance of being connected, being happy, and having fun in the store, which in turn feeds energy into the customer experience.

"When I'm out in stores in my district," says Carla, "I get a chance to see a lot of different partners. I try to set a playful and fun tone as I clean the toilets and scrub the drains and do all the things they do every day. If I can make a difference for them while I am there and do so in a fun way, they can come in the next day and give that type of service to our customers." In a sense, it is just as important to create an experience for employees as it is for employees to create an experience for customers. Facilitating a playful workplace keeps work teams engaged and motivated to do their best.

In addition to demonstrating playfulness by leadership example, Starbucks managers motivate partners simply by taking the time to recognize the partners' accomplishments. Sadly, this critical detail is often missed by business leaders. Starbucks management encourages and nurtures a playful, positive culture by opening up formal and spontaneous avenues to acknowledge and praise the company's people. District manager Amy Tingler reports, "One of the things we do with our partners is recognize great *Green Apron Book*–type interactions they have with customers and with one another. We celebrate those in front of the other partners during monthly meetings. For us, playful recognition is offered not just in terms of customer service, but also in how our people treat one another, in and outside the store."

Amy observed and acknowledged "a partner who, while working in the store, looked out the window and saw a regular customer standing by her car, visibly upset. That partner went out and asked the customer if everything was okay, and she told him she had locked her keys in her car. The partner went back into the store, grabbed a cordless phone and a phone book and made the woman her usual beverage. Going back outside, he told her he hoped things would get better and gave her the drink, phone, and phone book to make needed calls. She hadn't even entered the store, but he noticed her need. He took the initiative to go outside, welcome her, and genuinely respond to her plight. On an ensuing day, I went into his store early in the morning, wrote out a recognition card, explained the story to his colleagues, and thanked him in front of his team. It was a great way for all of us to start the day."

The culture of recognition at Starbucks doesn't take place only at the store manager and district manager levels. President and CEO Jim Donald starts each day making recognition calls to partners in stores throughout the world. While visiting the Starbucks Support Center, I observed the chairman of the board, Howard Schultz, casually and unobtrusively walk up to a partner's desk expressly to thank him for his effort on a project.

When the CEO and the chairman of the board value and practice appreciation, a culture typically develops in which people catch one another doing things right, thereby reinforcing desired behaviors and celebrating excellence. When a commitment to recognition is combined with a playful leadership spirit, employees tend to be engaged and happy. In turn, that satisfaction produces untold benefits in the development of positive interactions for coworkers and customers. Through those types of interactions, customer loyalty increases, and ultimately sales rise—a welcome outcome for any company. While some business executives don't appreciate the true impact of creating a positive culture, Starbucks success alone should be proof that where there is detailed attention to recognition, training, and play, there is profit.

All That and So Much More

What's left for Starbucks management to worry about, once they have attended to the details of the in-store environment, product quality, ongoing training, and the creation of a play-ful culture? The answer, as you might have guessed, is "every-thing." Many managers don't track details other than those that affect the quality of their product or service and their company's physical environment. But Starbucks leaders extend the Everything Matters orientation well beyond local and regional considerations. They apply their detail-oriented approach to worldwide environmental and social issues, even when a great percentage of their customer base may not real-ize that they are behaving with a global mind-set. So why would they be so broadly focused? In short, it's because supe-rior corporate leadership demands tireless excellence and a broad scope.

That excellence is reflected in the development of the Star-bucks paper cup sleeve. In August 1996, Starbucks and the Alliance for Environmental Innovation entered into a part-nership to reduce the environmental impact of serving coffee in the retail stores. At the time, many coffee drinkers required double (i.e., nested) cups to make their hot beverage easier to carry. In order to address environmental goals and maintain the customers' comfort, an arduous process was initiated to come up with a workable alternative.

Market research was conducted to look at the environ-mental impact of double-cupping. Two years of exploration was devoted to developing a quality hot cup that would allow for single-cupping, and the process resulted in an interim solution—a corrugated paper cup sleeve that Starbucks devel-oped. Other, more permanent solutions were attempted, and focus groups were brought in to analyze various options.

After considerable time and expense, the Starbucks Coffee Company/Alliance for Environmental Innovation Joint Task Force ultimately concluded in April 2000, "After more than two years of testing and developing prototypes of this cup, the data did not clearly indicate that the final version would meet all the criteria and could be brought to market within a reasonable time and cost. In addition, Starbucks customers had become accustomed to using a single paper cup with a corrugated paper sleeve."

All that extra effort was expended for a cup that will never reach the hand of a customer. Ouch! So, the single cup and sleeve remain, despite all attempts to produce a solo cup that could stand up to the heat. But even then, Starbucks management did not lose sight of its environmental objectives; it continued to champion improvements, such as changing the paper content of the cups to include 10 percent recycled materials. That attention to often unseen details led Starbucks to be the first company to achieve a cup that addressed environmental concerns.

So why do Starbucks managers care about research on paper cups? What's in it for them? The answer is amazingly simple: the Starbucks brand, and every company's brand, is nothing more than the sum total of the individual actions its people take. While some efforts may seem more publicly important than others, all actions (even the below-deck ones) are critical. In fact, companies that take a leadership position on environmental and social issues increasingly find that people are taking notice.

Customers like Lynn in Belleville, Michigan, gravitated to Starbucks exclusively because of its attention to detail on broader social concerns. "I don't drink coffee, so I never thought much about Starbucks. However, I heard they had an environmental mission statement that suggested that they were committed to environmental leadership in every aspect of their business."

Lynn continues, "I decided to read about their business practices and even talked to a partner who was amazingly passionate about social issues. All of this got me fired up, and I started volunteering at a store selling only Fair Trade items. Coincidently, my volunteer location is across the street from a Starbucks store. So every week when I go to my volunteer activity, I stop by Starbucks. I drink their tea because I like what the company stands for."

For Lynn and many other customers like her, the attention that Starbucks leadership gives to broad social issues gives the company a great advantage over its competitors. Most business leaders can strengthen the emotional connections between their company and their customers by listening to the community issues that are of greatest concern to those customers. By exploring what customers value and striving to have a positive effect in those areas of interest, Starbucks leadership has struck a strong emotional chord with the company's rapidly growing and strongly loyal customer base.

Everyone Matters—Uniqueness of Customers and Employees

Many customers are attentive to the smallest details, and at times business executives have to marvel at what catches the consumer's eye. Often customers are so discerning that no amount of money spent on advertising and marketing will make up for failed execution on the little things. Smoke, mirrors, and dazzle can fool some of the people some of the time, but an Everything Matters approach to some of the most mundane details wins customer loyalty and gets noticed in the strangest ways.

Customer Mara Siegler illustrates how the smallest and seemingly most basic details matter. "There are several problems particular to New York," she says, but "perhaps the gravest and most physically unbearable is the shortage of public restrooms. No matter where I find myself in the city, there is sure to be a Starbucks within a five-block radius. And to their credit, Starbucks bathrooms are usually clean. Business analysts, marketing gurus, and competing businesses can study the rise of this conglomerate all they want and give a billion reasons for its success. But trust me, no matter what the music, the flavor of the day, or the wireless availability, Starbucks success is all thanks to the free and clean toilets." Customers notice the little things—even the cleanliness of the bathrooms. It's important, therefore, for every business to ask its customers for feedback on the details that matter most to them. Often the answers to such questions give leadership the opportunity to master details of which they would otherwise have been unaware.

Not only must leaders be given the task of exploring the details that matter most to customers, but they must also explore what matters to their staff. If leaders understand what matters to employees, it is easier to excite and motivate those employees to give consistent effort—even in the less enjoyable aspects of their jobs. Barista Bernadette Harris confesses, "I didn't like making Frappuccinos®. I wasn't always happy to leave my line of hot drinks to make a drink that took twice as long! One customer helped me gain a different view of the blended beverages. This woman would come in every evening and order a mocha Frappuccino® blended beverage. She was always in a hurry, and we would barely converse. One evening she came in and mentioned that her husband was in the car. Then she thanked us for always delivering the drink in such a nice way and said that though she personally never drank Starbucks, it was the only thing her husband could stomach after his chemotherapy."

The trick for management, therefore, is to get employees to see the bigger picture and understand that small components of their day-to-day tasks can actually have a transformational impact on customers and the people with whom they work, not to mention on the company's overall mission and reputation.

When staff members execute details consistently, they are often rewarded by unexpected appreciation from customers. Regional director Carla Archambault tells about a barista, Susan, who was moving to another store. "As is often the case with our partners," explains Carla, "Susan was getting flowers from customers on her last day. While working at that store, Susan had made a commitment to try to get a particular customer, who could best be described as a grumpy guy, to smile. It might seem like a little thing, but to Susan it was important. Susan said, 'I don't know what's going on in this man's life, but I'm going to make him happy.' And so she would always connect and have a smile on her face, but he never smiled or showed any joy in response to her efforts."

"On the day Susan was leaving," continued Carla, "that man overheard that it was her last day. He came back before her shift was over and brought her a card. The words in the card were powerful; they read, 'I just want you to know how much it's meant for me to come into your store every day. I want you to know that I came in here specifically to see your smile and that you made a difference in my life.'" Susan took the time to do the little things necessary to demonstrate that this challenging customer mattered to her.

Susan's behavior is consistent with a resounding leadership message that is prevalent at Starbucks, namely, that not only does everything matter, but "everyone matters" as well. Accordingly, partners are reminded to master the details necessary to live the Five Ways of Being. This effort ensures that everyone, not just the highest-paying or most loyal customers, knows that he or she matters from the moment he or she arrives at a Starbucks store.

Former store manager and current Starbucks licensed store operations specialist Kimberly Kelly shows the impact this everything-and-everyone-matters approach can have. "There was a wonderful regular customer," says Kimberly, "in her seventies, named Irene, who had been a teacher and a principal. She and her husband visited daily—coming to Starbucks was an event for them. The husband always had on a sport jacket, she was dressed very elegantly, and they would order the same thing: a tall coffee and an extra cup so they could split it. They'd also order one muffin and two forks and a knife to share that as well. The couple would take their coffee and their muffin, and they would go slowly over to their table and spend maybe an hour or so visiting with each other and enjoying their time together."

Kimberly said the couple stopped coming into Starbucks, and she worried about them. One day she ran into Irene at a bank, and Irene shared that her husband had died of a sudden heart attack. Kimberly encouraged Irene to join her back at Starbucks after she finished her banking. Kimberly continued, "Irene came to my store, and when she approached the counter, she stood there and said, 'Kimberly, I just don't know what to order because we always shared items.' I simply said, 'You know what, I'm going to share that cup of coffee and that muffin with you today.' We sat down and talked

77

for about 30 minutes. She told me about how she missed her husband and how hard it was for her to move on. A few days later, Irene came back to my store. She was dressed in a beautiful outfit. She said, 'I'm ready to do this by myself now.' Irene asked if she could order a smaller cup of coffee. She took the muffin, one fork this time, and the knife. She split the muffin and told me, 'I guess I'll just have to make it last for two days.'"

So is it the coffee, the music, the couches, the relaxed pace, the smiles, or the free bathrooms? At Starbucks, it's attention to the details of everything—because everything matters. The details that are important to customers are as varied as the customers a business serves. But one thing is incontrovertible: when a company helps its people bring pride, excellence, and playfulness to every aspect of their jobs, those workers literally have the chance to change the lives of those around them.

Create Your Own Experience

- What should matter to you that may have been overlooked?

- What details could you attend to that probably matter to your colleagues and your business's customers?

- What small stuff needs your attention?

- Have you asked your customers what details matter to them?

- What can you do to help drive an everything-and-everyone-matters approach in your workplace?

- Whose life can you change?

Ideas to Sip On

Retail is detail. For that matter, all business is detail.

- Missed details produce dissatisfied customers who go elsewhere.

- A small detail is sometimes the difference between success and failure. Something as simple as a 7-cent valve helped Starbucks become a publicly traded company.

- Important details live in both that which is seen and that which is unseen by the customer.

- There really is no way to hide poor quality.

- Store environment, product quality, training, the development of a playful culture, and a social conscience all matter.

- Details affect the emotional connection (the "felt sense") that others have with you.

- Ask customers what details they notice about your business.

- Acknowledge, celebrate, and play!

- Not only does everything matter; everyone matters as well.

surprise and delight

"I slept and dreamt that life was joy.
I awoke and saw that life was service.
I acted and behold, service was joy."

—RABINDRANATH TAGORE

The idea behind the Surprise and Delight principle isn't a new one. In fact, one of the most famous commercial examples is more than a hundred years old. In the late 1800s at the World's Columbian Exposition, Chicago's first World's Fair, the Rueckheim brothers delighted young and old with their unique confection consisting of popcorn, peanuts, and molasses. While Cracker Jack® was a consistently popular treat, its appeal increased dramatically in 1912, when a surprise could be found in every package.

Businesses today are increasingly being challenged to provide the caramelized popcorn and peanuts as well as the "prize." Consumers want the predictable and consistent, with an occasional positive twist or added value thrown in. Psychologists who study happiness (the correct psychological/ research term is *subjective well-being*) often talk about the importance of predictability for safety and security (the caramelized popcorn, if you will), mixed with small increments of variety to offset boredom (the prize).

Unfortunately, many companies focus too much on the basic ingredients and not enough on adding that extra *something* that differentiates them from their competition and builds brand loyalty. Starbucks leaders, however, have made a firm commitment to creating an experience of Surprise and Delight in many areas of their business. Starbucks management seeks ways to implement subjective well-being for customers and staff—which, in turn, has a profound effect on loyalty, community, and profit.

The Expectation Effect

When Cracker Jack® made its debut, customers were truly surprised. But much has changed in a hundred years, and today's consumers are far more discerning and far harder to please. To complicate matters further, customers have developed a seemingly insatiable desire for the unique and amazing. Thanks to technologies and innovations that seemed impossible only a few short years ago, we have come to live in an age of "I gotta have it now, and it better be great."

Today, most of us expect a Cracker Jack®–like prize in just about everything we buy, from televisions (high definition), to tiny phones that double as cameras, to talking cars that tell us when to make the next right turn. Most consumers have such a high threshold for what constitutes a cutting-edge product that they thumb their noses at almost anything that doesn't "blow them away." We all seem to be waiting for the new wrinkle, the twist, the unexpected magical prize at the bottom of some sticky box.

Although it's a bit counterintuitive, leaders understand that even satisfied customers are looking for their purchases to offer more pleasure, joy, or play. People want more zing, but not necessarily a full-blown production. Starbucks leadership shows how any business can accomplish this mix of the expected and the unexpected. In the process, it demonstrates that you can and must remain true to the spirit and values of your company.

When a Business "Gets It"

Customers naturally expect businesses to respond to their needs when they are making routine requests during normal business hours. However, when a business defies the traditional, when it "colors outside the lines," customers often receive exceptional experiences. It is this type of nontradi-

83

tional approach that surprised Michael Cage as he pulled an all-nighter for a work project. As he writes on his "Marketing and Entrepreneurship" blog, at 5 a.m. Michael decided that it was time to get out of his house and take a break. His first thought was to reward himself with a predictable favorite, a vanilla latte. He hopped in his car and drove to his local Starbucks, anticipating his treat the whole way.

"As I pulled up to the store," he explains, "I knew something was terribly wrong; the sign was still dark, and the lights were off inside. I stopped the car and went up to the door to look at the hours. It was an hour before they opened, so I turned around to walk back to my car and figured the coffee would have to wait. . . . And then the lock was thrown, the door flew open, and one of my regular baristas stepped out and asked me whether I wanted something to drink." As Michael says, "Starbucks 'gets it.'"

While no company, including Starbucks, gets it right every time, Michael's barista certainly "got it" that time. His barista's decision to open the doors cost Starbucks nothing and gained it everything—a customer for life! For Michael, it was the surprise in his box of caramelized popcorn, a surprise that enhanced his already positive relationship with the brand.

Like Michael's, most positive unexpected events are natural and spontaneous, not artificial or forced. There is a need, and—BAM—someone steps in and fills it. Strangely, many customer needs are never actually stated, but determining them doesn't require psychic ability. It's just a matter of being open and attentive. That ability to anticipate the surprises that customers will enjoy is simply a part of Starbucks service-minded corporate culture.

A perfect example of this comes from a neighborhood library branch that was relocating. A number of librarians from that branch were daily customers at a nearby Starbucks. When the Starbucks manager found out about the relocation, she decided that she would buy the librarians coffee and take it to them at their new branch. She also found the closest Starbucks store to the new library and introduced the librarians to the baristas at that store. Leadership sets the tone for the importance of anticipating needs and surprising those whom the business serves.

Whether it's brewing coffee, designing software, or mopping floors, a commitment to Surprise and Delight literally transforms the very nature of work. Employment stops being about the words written in job descriptions and expands to include offering unexpected experiences.

These unexpected experiences occur often in a company like Starbucks, which is rich with employees who are looking to give customers positive surprises. Dr. Peter Nicholls, a British professor of cell and molecular biology, found this to be true when he slipped and fell in the street outside a Starbucks in Kuala Lumpur while running during a rainstorm. Three Starbucks partners—a store manager and two female baristas—weren't *just* serving coffee that day; they were seizing opportunities. The manager saw Peter fall, and he raced out to help. He and his team got other partners to cover their store, hailed a cab, took Peter to a clinic, and stayed with him while he was being treated.

Since Peter had left most of his money at his hotel earlier in the day, the store manager initially paid for Peter's care and got him medication and a sling for his injured arm. As Peter puts it, "They clearly worked together in an astonishing way. At least one of the baristas had just finished work, but there wasn't any issue about her jumping in to help. She could have said, 'I'm not on duty. I'm going home.' But she didn't. She stayed with me."

Michael, the librarians, and Peter all experienced welcome surprises because committed employees did the unexpected for them. But surprises don't have to be spontaneous. In many cases, the most powerful surprises are those that are planned.

A regular Starbucks customer, Mary, shares an experience of a well-organized surprise—the kind of event that takes advance planning to pull off successfully. Mary went into Starbucks on April 15 . . . *Tax Day*! She was stressed. She had just mailed what seemed like an overly generous payment to the IRS when she encountered an unexpected corporate Starbucks promotion.

As Mary put it, "Like I should be spending any money at all, I went into Starbucks to take my mind off my suffering. I walked up to the counter and told my barista, Thomas, that I wanted a cup of tea. He asked if I wanted Calm™ tea, causing me to wonder exactly how frazzled I looked. When I said, 'Calm™ would be good,' he said, 'Great, because today Starbucks is offering a free cup of Calm™ to all customers.'" Mary adds, "Okay, the Calm™ tea didn't wash away my IRS pain, but to this day I remember that drink. They didn't have to give me the tea, but they organized the event, and I benefited." The difference between good and great can often be the willingness of leadership to structure surprising moments around calendar opportunities.

For the most part, great surprises occur in our lives and the lives of our customers when someone, or some group of people, does something unexpected. It's not the "required" surprise fortieth birthday party; it's the occasional note to a client or colleague for no other reason than that he was in your thoughts. It's not a calculated marketing strategy; it's just the little things people do when they take the time to care.

Starbucks leadership often initiates a surprise event that is not primarily aimed at self-promotion. For example, on one occasion, Starbucks partners surprised customers in their stores with a product you can't even buy there. To celebrate summer and National Ice Cream Month, baristas served one million free cups of ice cream at 6,000 Starbucks locations for an unadvertised "ice cream social." Even though Starbucks sells ice cream in supermarkets, it doesn't sell it in its stores. So to make this event happen, ice cream was sent to stores via FedEx overnight delivery.

The ice cream social was simply an opportunity to treat customers. Starbucks leadership sees great value in creating positive surprises, as evidenced by the effort involved in orchestrating the complexities of an ice cream social. And this extra effort definitely worked to get the attention of customers. Martta Rose appreciated the ice cream, saying, "I never expected to get ice cream at Starbucks. It was wonderful, probably the best ice cream I've ever had. It was a nice break from the day."

The event also succeeded in bringing in people who had no plans to visit Starbucks that day. Jill Davis admitted, "I was actually leaving my job at a rival coffee shop across the street, and I was walking home. A Starbucks barista was standing outside handing out samples of the ice cream to passersby. I am a Starbucks fan—as well as an ice cream fan—so I accepted the barista's offer and enjoyed it on the rest of my walk home. How great is that?"

Create Your Own Experience

- When was the last time you were pleasantly surprised by a business?

- What memories do you have of unexpected extras that you've encountered as a customer or as a staff member? Were those surprises preplanned or spontaneous?

- What can you do to positively surprise a coworker, a customer, or some other unsuspecting recipient?

- Whom can you partner with to deliver surprises?

- What naturally occurring opportunities are ripe for creating surprise experiences?

There is no cookie-cutter approach to surprising customers (or colleagues, for that matter). It is not one size fits all. It doesn't have to be only about playful acts like ice cream socials. Genuine and meaningful gestures are all it takes. The most authentic surprises are often tied in with the company's regular products or services. For example, Starbucks gave out free books of poetry written by authors from the countries where coffee comes from: Indonesia and countries in Africa and Latin America.

Celebrating artists from these countries gave the company a unique way to share information on where various coffees were grown, while at the same time heightening the customers' experience in the stores. Appreciation came from people like Nadyne, a teacher, who captured the essence of a great surprise when she said, "This poetry touched me. I have shared it with friends. What's more, I have told many people

I know about it. You see, I came for the coffee. I will stay because the company offered me something I never really expected to find as a customer. They offered me thoughtfulness and joy."

Surprises are also a great way to introduce a new product or service in a way that requires little effort or money. A prime example comes from customer Moira Stevenson: "It was a Sunday afternoon ritual. My best friend and I would meet at our neighborhood Starbucks and talk about our latest dramas. This Sunday was no different—it was what happened as we finished our lattes that made it special. As we got up from our table, a Starbucks employee was walking around the room with a tray of little cups filled with an iced beverage. A new Frappuccino® blended beverage had just been introduced for the summer, and free samples were being distributed in order to celebrate.

"We gladly accepted our samples and, upon looking around the room, realized that our favorite Starbucks had been transformed into a mini-cocktail party. Instantly the café was not only filled with the regulars, but also buzzed with conversation and a common bond—the drink. It was nice that we all stopped what we were doing and socialized with one another." Here, the introduction of a new product actually became an event that encouraged customers to try something new in a nonintimidating way.

Customers can experience pleasure from something as simple as an unexpected exchange of information. Duane, a fairly new customer to Starbucks, makes the point: "I was at a music-listening bar at a local Starbucks. I had never seen one before. A barista took the time to show me how I could listen to all this music for free. I got to hear whole songs from artists I'd never run into. I totally lost track of time. I was in there for three hours drinking coffee and listening to music, and all the music listening was free. Unbelievable!" Duane's reaction was rather strong, since all he received was a few music-listening tips from a partner. But that small amount of help turned into hours of enjoyable discovery and surprise for Duane.

While information can enhance positive customer experiences, introducing an element of play into regular day-to-day (and often commonplace) activities can also achieve memorable results. Regular Starbucks customer Brad Montgomery is a motivational humorist by profession and therefore is very aware of those rare instances when people engage one another with playfulness. Brad encountered the light-hearted spirit of one Starbucks barista who made an ordinary coffee-buying experience something far more meaningful.

According to Brad, "I was chatting with the woman behind the counter at Starbucks. She was just a fun person with a big smile. When she gave me back my credit card, she held it out for me to take back. But here was the great part: when I grabbed it, she didn't let go. I pulled, but she hung on. I looked up and met her eyes, and bingo! A huge smile was on her face. She was doing it. She was using this tiny bit of humor on the job to inject a playful moment into our day. Humor in the workplace? You bet! She proved that adding or creating a smile or two here and there can turn a day around. And if you string enough of those days together . . ."

As Brad's experience illustrates, simple acts often create the greatest connection between people. Ira Shull, a customer from Shirley, Massachusetts, tells of a time when genuine interest took him by surprise. "This past summer my wife and I were visiting Seattle," he explains, "and I wanted to get my morning coffee and get back to the hotel as quickly as possible. So I walked into this Starbucks and stood in line with a bunch of men in suits and ties, my gym shorts almost hanging down to my flip-flops. I got to the counter and was about to place my order when the barista, a young guy with a goatee, asked, 'How was your weekend?'"

"My mouth hung open, and a low, burbling sound came out," continues Ira. "I had expected a mundane question, not this kind of familiar, and dare I say intimate, opener between two confidantes. I was impressed, as I believe civility and politeness are two important things missing from our lives these days. All I could come up with for an answer was, 'I'm not from around here.'

"The barista immediately asked, 'Oh, where are you from?'" And, Ira comments, "He actually sounded sincere, which I found hard to believe. I explained where I lived and what we had been doing on our vacation, and we had a nice conversation. As I was putting my cream in my coffee, a woman who had overheard my discussion with the barista joined in and all three of us chatted amiably. Both she and the barista began giving me tips on what to see in Seattle. I felt oddly happy. Even if it had been a little nothing conversation, I had made a brief connection with people in passing whom I would probably never see again. Whenever that happens, at a Starbucks or anywhere else, it's always a pleasant surprise."

Rather than encouraging trite customer service sayings like "Have a nice day" or other scripted communications, successful leaders help staff look for genuine opportunities to do the positively unexpected. Whether it is in the service of customers, coworkers, or suppliers, the willingness to take a genuine interest in another person is often among the most pleasant surprises of all.

Unconventional Surprises Are Often the Best

Senior Starbucks management understands that one of the greatest things about surprises is that they are original. You can find them anywhere, which has the added benefit of allowing you to offer them to current customers, future customers, and even people who would never have anticipated being in your place of business. Surprises can go where you find people, *not* just where people find you.

Such "traveling surprises" also provide an opportunity to reach what management guru Peter Drucker called "noncustomers." A group of district managers decided to organize a citywide coffee tasting. According to one of the managers, "We called it a citywide coffee break. We had 10 Coffee Masters, partners who are certified based on their knowledge of the coffee, the growing process, the processing, and so forth, actually go to the train station and set up a table. We gave away free coffee to all the commuters—everybody getting on a train, everybody getting off a train. People were surprised, and it was a great opportunity for us, too. . . . We were celebrating Fair Trade Certified™ coffee; Starbucks was one of the first companies in the United States to offer this product."

The main goal of the giveaway was to surprise and celebrate. As a result, the commuters were offered a pleasant experience that was not used as a gimmick to get them into Starbucks stores. One of the district managers at the event explains, "We didn't try to sell Starbucks. We just wanted to do something fun and enjoyable, although I imagine that through the process, some people may have learned about our involvement with Fair Trade Certified™ coffee, our commitment to support the farmers, and that we take social issues seriously."

The power of that day for Starbucks partners and train passengers alike came from the totally unexpected nature of the event. It was not some publicity stunt announced with glitzy ads. The free coffee simply fell into the hands of unexpecting commuters. Who would have thought that any business would seek to surprise people as they went about their everyday routines?

While the train station coffee giveaway was not primarily intended for publicity, Starbucks has used surprise as part of its advertising campaigns. In a couple of instances, rather than simply buying billboard space, Starbucks placed regular-size magnetic coffee cups on the tops of cabs. To the unsuspecting observer, it looked as if a cup had been left there accidentally. Cab drivers were also involved in the surprise. They were to give Starbucks gift cards to individuals who advised the driver that the cup was there. This novel idea created an interactive relationship between the advertisement (namely, the magnetic cup) and the Good Samaritans who noticed it and took the time to be helpful.

Starbucks leadership not only directs surprises at customers and potential customers, but extends them to partners as well. In 2004, for example, Starbucks partners (who met basic criteria, such as having worked 500 hours during the year) were treated to an unexpected $250 holiday bonus. Jim, a barista in Washington, D.C., reacts: "I have never worked for a company in the food or service industry that gave all the lowest-level employees a bonus of this much money. Realize that this bonus was *not* for the store managers and above; rather, it was for the baristas and shift supervisors. These are the folks who work hard every day making lattes for people."

When leaders care enough to surprise their staff, employee morale soars, and important modeling takes place. Not only do employees engage themselves more passionately in their

93

work, but they also become energized. That energy is infectious, and people both inside and outside the company benefit from the enthusiasm.

Create Your Own Experience

- In what ways have you been surprised in your workplace?

- How can you surprise others through small gestures or tokens of appreciation?

- What energy have you expended to understand the ways in which your colleagues like to be surprised?

- How can you remind yourself to bring surprise into the lives of others?

- What benefits can you expect from enhancing your ability to create positive, unexpected experiences at work?

Not only can unexpected events be used to create a positive and dynamic culture, but they can also encourage unusual partnerships. An amazing example of this occurred when a Starbucks partner worked with other employees and members of her community to share their love of Starbucks coffee with soldiers halfway around the globe.

A month prior to being deployed to the rugged mountains of Afghanistan, Sergeant Scott Matthews, a Black Hawk helicopter mechanic and national guardsman, purchased an espresso machine and some coffee from an Atascadero, California, Starbucks. Sergeant Matthews' sister-in-law, Amy Mueller, a barista at this location, not only arranged for shipping and delivery of the machine, but worked through her store manager, customers, and other Starbucks partners to provide twice-monthly shipments of free coffee to Bagram, Afghanistan.

As Amy explains, "My job was to keep the supplies coming. It started with me telling a couple of regular customers about it, and they wanted to get involved. Later, I decorated a jar and got permission from my manager to put it on the pickup counter. Customers would put $20 bills in there; I was shocked. We collected about $450 in donations. One customer told me how important it was to remind our soldiers we were thinking of them. He and his kids made Christmas boxes and sent them to Afghanistan. We also supplied the soldiers with paper logo cups so it would have a real 'Starbucky' feel."

As luck would have it, one member of Sergeant Matthews's unit was actually a former Starbucks barista. Matthews and company opened a thriving makeshift Starbucks-like coffee shop at their base near the flight line. Sergeant Matthews comments, "You needed a special pass to travel into our vicinity, but people would come in with pass holders just to have our version of the Starbucks Experience." A Web site created for family members back home showed images of the coffee shop near the flight line, with a large Starbucks banner flying overhead.

When the media happened upon the Web site, military legal officials encouraged Matthews to consider shutting down the coffee operation for fear that it would violate Starbucks copyright protections. In the nick of time, David Silldorff, Military/ Government program manager for Starbucks, contacted Sergeant Matthews and supported the use of the Starbucks name at its unofficial Afghan location. Then David asked a magical question in the world of surprise and delight: "Is there

95

anything else you need?" Shortly thereafter, David sent a much-welcomed coffee grinder from the Starbucks Support Center.

Sergeant Matthews added, "I cannot tell you the joy this coffee shop brought us. It was a surprisingly wonderful taste of home. My fellow soldiers and I will be forever grateful to the baristas, the Atascadero store manager, Troy, and everyone at Starbucks for their support. I am also thankful for how that little shop gave many people an opportunity to contribute something to our efforts. One person sent a note along with a coffee donation that really caught me. It said, 'I've wanted to do something for you guys, but didn't know where to turn. Have a cup of coffee on me.'"

While barista Amy may have started the flow of coffee to Sergeant Matthews' Starbucks, she also gave many others an opportunity to pour their own energy in as well. Customers who participated in the project were able to share in the joy of helping others. As a result, those customers became uniquely involved with Starbucks and positively touched lives. When businesses partner with customers in these personal ways, they create a loyalty that is far greater than what a company could obtain by simply serving a high-quality product. Business leaders give their people the opportunity and permission to make a real connection with their customers.

As seen in train stations and the Afghanistan Starbucks, great surprises need not take place at a company's headquarters or in one of its stores or offices. In fact, some of the more meaningful and powerful ways to touch others—and reach new customers—is by surprising them in unconventional settings. Ultimately, by incorporating your brand into people's everyday lives, you are given an amazing opportunity to drive home the message that your company is not just routine, but exceptional.

Joy from Unexpected Sources

One of the great things about surprises is that their impact can be far-reaching. Once a business culture embraces the importance of generating joy, pleasing others takes on a life of its own. Not only do staff members surprise customers, but they also surprise one another. The coworkers of Bernadette Robinson, a Starbucks barista in Chicago, Illinois, were able to deliver a surprise of life-changing proportion when they enlisted the resources of one of the world's best-known celebrities.

Bernadette was a single mother of three whose family literally tripled in size overnight after she rescued her six nieces and nephews, who had been placed in state custody. Her Starbucks coworkers knew about Bernadette's huge heart and her small apartment, so they launched an all-out campaign to get the attention of Oprah Winfrey's television show producers. Unbeknownst to Bernadette, the other partners at the store did all they could to get Oprah to help their colleague. They aggressively bombarded Oprah with pleas on Bernadette's behalf. Ultimately, Oprah surprised Bernadette by showing up at the Starbucks counter where Bernadette worked! In response to Bernadette's colleagues' requests for assistance, Oprah provided a shopping spree for all the children in Bernadette's care and, more important, a new, furnished home for Bernadette and her family.

In a culture like Starbucks, where leaders surprise staff members and staff members surprise customers, it is no wonder that Bernadette's colleagues would seek to positively surprise her. What often goes unnoticed, however, is that this dynamic energy activates customers to surprise one another.

Barista Danielle states, "I was on drive-through, and one gentleman told me that he would like to buy the next person's drink. That person decided to keep the surprise going by paying for the drinks of the car behind him. This went on for 11 cars; everyone was touched, and I was about in tears." Surprise and delight over and over again, for 11 cars in a row. But 11 cars is nothing compared to one Starbucks drive-through that reported 33 consecutive cars' worth of similar surprise moments. Jim Alling, president of Starbucks U.S. Business, noted at a shareholders' meeting that these "pay-it-forward" stories reflect how surprise and delight can all start from the actions of a Starbucks partner simply "over a cup of coffee."

Starbucks creates surprise experiences. Those experiences represent the prize that keeps its partners engaged and its customers returning. But what about the caramelized popcorn? That's where consistency and delight come in!

Create Your Own Experience

- From your most loyal customer to an absolute stranger, how can you create an experience of surprise?

- Surprise can occur spontaneously or with a well-developed plan, playfully and meaningfully. What will resonate most with the people around you?

- What's your investment to serve up joy and the unexpected?

- Look inside your company. How can you share your joy with employees or coworkers? How can you use surprise to give them the extra motivation they need to share that joy with others?

Delighting Your Customers

It has been said that the only two things one can count on are death and taxes. Wouldn't it be great if consistent quality and experience were an equally sure thing? Since consistency is rare and valued, companies that master it ultimately thrive.

Predictability produces customer delight. People are pleased when they know that a company will deliver what it promises. And even when something goes wrong, an employee or manager can still delight the customer by going the extra mile to make things right. Delight is the result of an unwavering commitment to creating a comfortable and trusted customer relationship.

Creating the Familiar: Predictability in Product

Great businesses deliver a quality product in a predictable manner. Starbucks executive Martin Coles is well aware of the importance of consistency. He emphasizes, "What we're really looking for is that you take your personal Starbucks experience—something we call the 'My Starbucks Experience'—as you travel, and have a good percentage of that experience no matter where you go. It's not the same partners serving you, but if the experience overall is similar enough, you will have that visceral connection with Starbucks. You'll be able to take a little bit of it home with you and have delight and comfort in that."

It's this consistency that is recognized by patrons from city to city and country to country. One such Starbucks customer is Paul Viapiano, a musician who has toured internationally with the Los Angeles Philharmonic and Hollywood Bowl Orchestra. As Paul points out, "Starbucks is really consistent no matter where you go in the world. I've been to Starbucks in Edinburgh, London, Tokyo . . . and they were all great. Starbucks is the traveler's best friend!"

By holding out a standard of legendary service, defining the five key ways to make that service happen, and communicating successes and breakdowns, Starbucks leadership links each individual store to a common objective. Consistency means that customers will find safety in the company, its product, and its service. They can trust Starbucks and incorporate it into important and special times in their lives. For regular customer Elif Wisecup, Starbucks serves an important grounding function in a whirlwind of travel.

"As a political consultant," says Elif, "my husband works hard in a job that he absolutely loves. He's constantly on planes, living in hotel rooms, and switching time zones as he attends focus groups, meets with candidates, and plans campaigns. He travels all over the country, and I often join him when my schedule allows or when I'm in danger of forgetting what he looks like!"

According to Elif, her husband's "first order of business is to locate a Starbucks. He's like a general establishing a base camp. No other location will do. Sure, he's staying at a hotel. Sure, he could start the day by eating a stale muffin from a continental breakfast display and by brewing himself a cup of coffee using the in-room machine with water from the bathroom sink. But the feeling of walking into a clean and bright Starbucks and being helped by friendly staff, no matter where you are, is more than worth the price of admission. The familiar surroundings provide a sense of continuity in our very discontinuous lives, and for that, we are grateful."

When others can rely on you to provide them with exactly what they expect no matter where they are, you reinforce the image and strength of your brand in the place that matters most: the minds and hearts of your customers. Your brand literally becomes the standard by which other companies are measured. For example, regular Starbucks customers who choose to visit other coffee providers run the risk that they will not get what they have come to expect and may feel disappointed when their experience "just isn't Starbucks."

With consistency comes customer trust. Consumers gain stability when they know that they can depend on having a reliable experience. For customer William Stewart, Starbucks provided the stabilizing force he needed to get through a challenging time. As he explains,

> *I recently had to take an emergency trip to Houston to visit my father, who had developed a heart condition while on a business trip and was in the hospital. The day of the flight was extremely stressful. When I finally got to the hospital and saw my father recovering, the next thing on my mind was Starbucks. I cannot tell you how calming it was to have a taste of home when I was many miles away.*

101

Consistency is crucial for success in a world that is unpredictable. Given interruptions, intrusive phone calls, and unexpected deadlines, most of us are looking for a familiar and comfortable refuge. Many find it in a morning cup of coffee from Starbucks; some secure it in the work of a favorite author; still others relish a few minutes of quiet time before bed. People come to trust that these sources of delight can be relied upon, both in their simplicity and in their constancy.

Creating Predictability in Experience

Predictability is difficult to achieve. We all know that it is hard to get comparable service from the same person two days in a row. Imagine the challenge for Starbucks. The leadership is attempting to ensure a consistent product and service every day in thousands of stores throughout the world. Starbucks knows that having a predictable, high-quality experience is a driving force behind the extremely high level of customer loyalty. For this reason, the highest priority is placed on creating memorable service, where customers are treated in ways that delight them.

All partners are instructed in the importance of delighting customers, especially those partners who have the most direct customer interaction. One barista explains, "I know Starbucks major focus is legendary service. Not just great, but legendary. The store I work for is not conveniently located, so the fact that we have so many regulars is due to our service standards. We also do our best to assure new customers that it's okay to try what we have, and that we'll do everything we can to fix their drink, or replace it, if they don't like it. A lot of other coffee shops I go into, and, indeed, have worked for, are staffed with uninterested college students, so coming into Starbucks, both as a customer and as an employee, was a sigh of relief to me."

By providing a high-quality, consistent customer experience, Starbucks offers a place for conversation, connection, and reconnection. For this reason, customers incorporate Starbucks into the rituals of their lives.

Erica from Sacramento, California, realized the important role Starbucks played in her life when her son's first words were, "Mommy, Starbucks." As she explains, "At first it would be a stop at Starbucks once or twice a week when out doing our morning errands, like grocery shopping or banking. Slowly, I realized I was going to the grocery store every other day. And to the bank on days I wasn't going to the grocery. Why, you ask? So that I could make that easy right-hand turn into Starbucks. And to appease my little toddler, I'd grab him a healthy bottle of juice. Soon, I realized that my son looked forward to this morning ritual just as much as I did."

Humans, by nature, look forward to ritual. Starbucks leadership understands that a business can become a part of customers' rituals and routines by offering a familiar experience. Professor & Minister Todd Bouldin says, "Go by Starbucks on any given afternoon, and you will find young people huddled around tables in conversation for hours. Business meetings take place. Friends catch up over a Frappuccino® blended beverage. The person behind the register comes to know us by name, and our name is even placed on our cup. It is safe, personal, and simple—to some extent, routine—and that seems to be what keeps drawing us back over and over again. Starbucks has found the favor of all the people."

When a business consistently draws the favor of a large number of people, other individuals gather at that location to enjoy community. For this reason, Reverend Josh Loudermilk, Liberty Hill UMC, has made Starbucks his church office: "I know Starbucks is trying to be the third place after home and work, but for me it's my second place—it *is* where I work. It's where the community gathers, so I respectfully gather there as well."

Starbucks has built its brand with far less advertising than most other companies of its size. When customers can rely on a consistent positive experience, they feel compelled to share their experience with others. This creates an ever-growing customer base through word of mouth. By being predictable, a business offers comfort, routine, reliability, and, in the case of Starbucks, a place where the community gathers.

Delighting Customers Even When Things Go Wrong

Mistakes happen. In business, what often matters most is how a company and its staff respond when a mistake is brought to their attention. Companies often hope that a mistake can be remedied in a way that salvages their relationship with the customer. But, what if the breakdown leads to a breakthrough that actually delights!

Starbucks leadership understands that unhappy customers represent opportunities to improve the experience. Gregg Johnson, Starbucks senior vice president of Emerging Businesses, notes, "While we don't always get the opportunity to have a second chance with a customer, occasionally people will let us know how we could have made their experience better. When that gift is given, we need to seize it. By examining an individual customer's dissatisfaction, we have a chance not only to regain the trust of that customer, but to more broadly fix a process that is likely affecting other customers as well."

For example, Starbucks encourages all partners to do what they can to please customers when their exact needs are not met. One customer, Darrick Rochili, reports, "I went to the Starbucks near my office to get a grande white chocolate mocha. The server told me that they were out of white chocolate. He asked if he could make me another drink. I asked for a regular mocha, and guess what? He told me that the drink would be on the house because they ran out of what I wanted. I say that's great customer service. I would have been okay without the free drink, but by doing this, Starbucks got a repeat customer who will spread good words about the company."

Sometimes staff members just don't know what they can do to help a customer, because they have limited options at their disposal. One customer who had purchased a quality French Press from Starbucks came into his local store expecting that he could purchase necessary replacement parts. His barista realized that she could not meet his expectation and that he would probably have to buy another French Press. After initially struggling to resolve his needs, the barista asked for the customer's patience as she tried to find an alternative solution.

As she puts it, "I told him that we didn't have any parts, so I ran into the back room to double-check with my manager [to ask] if I could just give him a new French Press even though his had been well used. . . . I came back and told him that I would be happy to exchange it for a new one. The look on his face was priceless. He kept asking me if I was sure, then said that he felt bad because he didn't come in to get a free one. I kept reassuring him that it was fine and it wouldn't be a problem to exchange it. After the exchange, he asked to speak to my manager. He was so impressed with our service that he wanted to know where he could send a letter or call to inform corporate. I could just tell that we had really made his day; it's a nice feeling!" Even when initial breakdowns occur, leaders help their teams find solutions that will delight others and maintain constructive long-term relationships.

Delight can also come from the staff attending to things that go wrong—on the *customer's* side of the relationship. Laura Vernier experienced this firsthand. A regular customer at Starbucks, she remembers stopping by her local store on one particularly rough day to order a grande sugar-free caramel Macchiato. When she realized she didn't have her wallet, the barista said, "It's okay, you look like you really need it. Pay next time." The result, says Laura, is that "the worst days of my life are so easily turned around the second I step into Starbucks."

If, at the end of each day, you and your colleagues have invested the extra energy to delight others rather than simply satisfy them, you will ultimately be rewarded with extraordinary results. Brad Stevens, vice president of Marketing at Starbucks, sums it up well: "By creating consistently intimate stores, we have become the living room of the neighborhood. We are not content to be liked. We want to be loved. We are not looking for romantic love or the love a mother has for a child. We are looking for that rare situation where people say, 'Oh, I love that company.' Or, 'I love that drink. I love those guys.' We want that sense of affinity. I know it's audacious to have that as a goal, to want to be a beloved company, but

Create Your Own Experience

- What can you do to enhance the predictability of your business, either on the product or on the service front?

- How can you ensure that your business delights customers more consistently and becomes a part of their routines and rituals?

- How can you achieve status as a beloved company?

- What can you do to turn break*downs* into memorable break*throughs* for your customers?

I think if any company can do it, we can. It's by sticking to those types of ways to interact with and delight customers that we'll ultimately get there."

Predictability, consistency, ritual, routine, community, and service recovery are key. If you and your business succeed at delighting every person you work with, you *will* be a beloved company, and in the process your customers will get both the caramelized popcorn and the prize.

Ideas to Sip On

Delight is the caramelized popcorn; surprise is the prize!

- Nowadays, people have a certain anticipation or hope that they will be dazzled, even in the most mundane experiences.

- The most effective events are natural and spontaneous, not artificial or forced. Look first for a need, and, BAM—step in and fill it.

- Surprise can be as simple as offering a little guidance and then getting out of the way as people search for things that bring them joy.

- Your efforts to surprise others are a contagious force.

- Customer delight comes from surprise as well as predictability.

- When breakdowns occur, businesses can still delight customers by making things right.

- Delight is the result of an unwavering commitment to creating a comfortable and trusted relationship.

embrace resistance

"Don't mind criticism. If it is untrue,
disregard it; if unfair, keep from irritation;
if it is ignorant, smile; if it is justified,
it is not criticism—
learn from it."

—AUTHOR UNKNOWN

The German poet Heinrich Heine once noted that a person "only profits from praise" when he "values criticism." Valuing criticism is a major piece of the Starbucks puzzle, and it plays a large role in the Embrace Resistance ingredient that is outlined in this chapter. Embracing resistance involves a complex set of skills that can enable businesses and individuals to create business and relationship opportunities when they are confronted with skepticism, irritation, or wariness.

This principle requires leaders to distinguish between customers who want their concerns to be resolved and those individuals who will never stop complaining or be satisfied. Embracing resistance involves more than simply placating people or groups that pose a challenge. It focuses on learning from individuals who don't always make it easy to listen.

In business, it is great to see your company's name in the press when things are going well. However, it is a decidedly different story when the media target your company in a negative fashion. Such was the case for Starbucks when a column written by David M. Martin, the chief training consultant for NCBS, appeared on Tom Brown's bankstocks.com Web site.

The column, titled "Wake Up and Smell the Latte," was an unsparing, detailed critique of service issues at Starbucks licensed stores.

As David notes, "The trait of Starbucks that has appealed to me the most in the past has begun to weaken. That trait is *consistency*. Simply, I think it was once extremely difficult to have a bad experience at a Starbucks. No matter what time of day or night, no matter what city you were in, no matter what product you purchased—*you could count on good service and that the product would taste like you expected it to taste.*

"These days, off the top of my head, I can give you two addresses of Starbucks close to my home in which you have at least a 50/50 chance of being unpleasantly surprised by the product or service. It's also telling that both of these locations are 'licensed' stores located within another retailer [emphasis added]."

David, who is considered a customer service expert in the banking industry, sums up his frustration by noting the following:

"One lesson I think we can all learn from this is that no brand is unassailable. I've heard scores of banks in the past mention Starbucks as an inspiration for well-branded, customer-pleasing stores. But even a phenomenon like Starbucks, with a large and devoted customer base, can develop cracks in its armor when its service levels lose consistency. And it's usually not a single, dramatic event that weakens a brand. Most often, it's a gradual erosion that can be explained away as a temporary issue or maybe 'growing pains.' Too often, the 'exception' of slightly lesser quality in time becomes the norm. The facilities look the same, but the customers' experiences slip [emphasis added]."

At a great many companies, such negative publicity might be dismissed as the opinion of an angry journalist or argued against by leaders who are unwilling to participate in open, candid self-exploration. Other corporate leaders might try to counteract the bad press by distracting customers with promotions or other gimmicks.

Starbucks management, on the other hand, has built a company on a willingness to actively listen to criticism. Therefore, complaints are addressed head on, as evidenced by what David Martin reported shortly after his negative Starbucks column was published:

"A few days after the column posted, I was in an airport, and picked up a voicemail message that caught my attention. The call was from a gentleman named Gregg Johnson . . . the SVP of Emerging Businesses at Starbucks. He stated that he had read the column and would appreciate the opportunity of discussing it with me. I think I cringed. . . .

"I was able to call Gregg that evening. I remember preparing myself for an unpleasant interaction. I know that many senior managers become über-defensive when given negative feedback. Nothing could have been further from the truth.

"To begin with, Gregg thanked me for my business. He then told me that he apologized for the instances in which his company had failed to deliver the kind of experiences they strive for and customers expect. In 10 seconds, he had turned this phone call into a pleasant one [emphasis added]."

Ultimately, David and Gregg developed a positive and ongoing relationship, and Gregg and other Starbucks leaders have spoken at events sponsored by David's organization. Gregg has even utilized David's initial critique as a training tool for partners in licensed stores.

From David's perspective,

The entire experience reinforced a few lessons for me:

1. *When presented with negative feedback by a customer, recognize that you may have an opportunity to* actually *strengthen that relationship. By first thanking customers for their business and recognizing their grievances, . . . you are far more likely to keep that customer as well as gain* useful feedback *to improve your business.*

2. *When employees see that* management actually cares *about feedback—positive and negative—they are more likely to care as well. When they see that management is personally committed to* addressing issues, repairing and/or solidifying relationships, *they will likely be more committed as well* [emphasis added].

When Gregg was asked why a senior vice president at Starbucks would take the time to respond to the author of a column on a banking Web site, he noted, "You respond because you can see the perspective of the customer, and you obviously respond to get customer recovery. But the main reason you take action is because it is an opportunity to learn more about what we can do, how we can be better, how we can approach things differently, how we can help our operators be better operators, how we can help our baristas be better baristas and customer service advocates, and how we, as leaders, can guide them more effectively toward the ultimate goal, which is to provide that great experience."

Gregg further explains that leaders should take feedback like that provided by David and "process it at the senior level and ask, are there enough data points in here that I should shift strategy, that I should alter an initiative, or that I should be looking at the business differently."

When these complaints are shared with other managers, strategies can be developed to fix commonly occurring breakdowns. Directing those same complaints back to front-line staff offers employees palpable data about how they also can be more effective.

As Gregg explains, "There is power in sharing the specific customer experiences with the folks down the line because of the learning that takes place. In the case of this article or any customer letter, the verbatim conversation, the voice of the customer that comes through is so much more powerful than any report that says that 42.5 percent of our customers are highly satisfied. The emotional connection that people make in reading the words of others or in hearing voice to voice the words of others has much more impact. It grabs their emotions and drives them to different behavior much more effectively than any statistical reporting will ever provide."

Through its history, Starbucks leadership has weathered significant storms of criticism, many of them more withering than that offered by David. But any public company that has grown as fast as Starbucks will inevitably become a lightning rod for controversy. Because of its media profile, its core values, and leaders like Gregg, Starbucks has developed a talent for embracing the resistance that has been directed its way. It has learned not to discount its critics and dissenters, but to listen for the learning opportunities that come through those voices.

At both the corporate and the individual partner levels, Starbucks managers have found ways to see possible lessons that can be gained from those who challenge them. By not only reacting to issues, but involving detractors in problem-solving discussions, Starbucks executives develop better solutions to business and social concerns. This process also earns the buy-in of those who may have otherwise opposed them.

Taking it one step further, Starbucks leadership has learned to troll for emerging issues and possible areas of resistance and apply resources to those areas early and proactively. When needed, Starbucks works diligently to correct misperceptions. When errors are made, leaders understand the importance of taking swift, unequivocal responsibility, and they follow that up with corrective action. What doesn't kill businesses does make them stronger, but only if their leadership heeds the lessons presented to them.

Macro Resistance

Nothing in nature grows without facing limiting forces. Seeds meet the resistance of the earth's crust. Trees are resisted by the wind. Animals are limited by other animals. Businesses and individuals, particularly those that grow and develop rapidly, meet the resistance of dynamic market and social forces. Starbucks has expanded at an almost unheard-of rate. That growth, coupled with its open public access, has put its leadership face to face with much opposition and has frequently placed the company in the middle of many social challenges.

Although Starbucks buys approximately 4 percent of all coffee sold worldwide, the company typically draws greater public scrutiny than far larger coffee buyers who sell their product primarily in supermarkets. When issues regarding commitment to purchase Fair Trade Certified™ coffee surface, the evening news is likely to show a protest in front of a Starbucks store. In truth, the larger buyers of commodity and noncommodity coffee have more influence on international buying practices than Starbucks has, but those companies seldom have to endure the harsh glare of the media spotlight. Although Starbucks leads the industry in attempting to create positive change for farmers, it rarely receives acknowledgment for being one of North America's largest roasters and retailers of Fair Trade Certified™ coffee or the only company certified to sell Fair Trade Certified™ coffee in 21 countries.

Because there is so much emotional energy swirling around Starbucks—both favorable and unfavorable—journalist Jim Romenesko decided to develop a blog site, www.starbucks gossip.com, where customers, baristas, and others who are interested in Starbucks can react to news articles about the company. Jim reports Web traffic of approximately 5,000 visitors per day, noting, "There are few companies about which you could create a site like this. Starbucks has a truly loyal following with strong emotional reactions to the company. I can't see putting up a subwaysandwichgossip.com site and people caring that much about it."

Despite the fact that people are very vocal about Starbucks, its leadership frequently takes an accepting and respectful approach to the views of others. For example, Starbucks management has not sought to influence or encourage a positive spin on the information shared on Jim's site. According to Jim, he has functioned completely independently of Starbucks. Jim notes,

"The *Wall Street Journal* did a story, and the reporter asked Starbucks what the policy was concerning looking at Web sites related to the company, and the response was something like, 'We have no policy for monitoring Web sites.' I see that as consistent with some of its other hands-off policies. For example, the fact that I sit for maybe five hours in a Starbucks with one drip coffee doesn't bother the company at all. It's just a 'leave them be' attitude, and it extends to my Web site and then to my coffee shop habits as well."

In a business environment in which many corporate leaders strictly monitor every outgoing brand message—and sometimes threaten legal action when an outsider tinkers with their image—Starbucks executives have instead successfully built their brand by generating an often more relaxed approach.

Create Your Own Experience

- Where have you missed opportunities to strengthen relationships with others by simply listening to their discontent?

- How gracefully do you model a willingness to embrace resistance and accept responsibility?

- In what ways can you use the criticism directed at your company to improve your functioning or that of your team?

For some concerns, listening is all that is required. It offers space for commentary and constructive discussion. Other types of resistance demand direct action. Great leaders know when listening is not enough.

Starbucks leadership took immediate action when social concerns about the living conditions and environmental practices in many third world coffee-growing countries began to surface. According to Dub Hay, senior vice president of Coffee and Global Procurement, "Rather than ignoring the voices of those who expressed concern about the way migrant coffee pickers are treated or the environmental practices of coffee farmers, our people in the Coffee Department began working with socially conscious groups that were among the most vocally critical. In conjunction with these organizations and Conservation International, Starbucks staff members developed socially responsible coffee-buying guidelines called C.A.F.E. (Coffee and Farmer Equity) Practices. These guidelines are designed to help our coffee buyers work with coffee farmers to ensure high-quality product and promote equitable relationships with farmers, workers, and communities, as well as protect the environment."

Whereas many corporate executives dread dealing with complaints, Starbucks management actually invites dissenters in for problem-solving discussions. Because Starbucks leadership is sensitive to issues of globalization, and given that its customers feel strongly about the company's being a good steward of human and environmental resources, Starbucks executives sought to create a program that rewarded best practices for coffee growers in the third world, where most of its coffee is purchased.

To put it simply, you can't argue with the results of this engaging approach. C.A.F.E. Practices offer higher coffee contracts when producers demonstrate improvement and excellence on 26 separate criteria involving the environment, coffee quality, and social living standards. These improvements are verified by independent evaluators. Rather than rolling out the program in a haphazard way, Starbucks piloted it for two years, making constant improvements. (More details on the C.A.F.E. Practices program can easily be found at the Starbucks Web site, www.starbucks.com.) Above all, lives have been greatly improved through the willingness of Starbucks leadership to welcome critics into the development of real-world solutions.

Starbucks executives clearly do not suffer from an "ostrich syndrome," burying their heads in the sand when faced with criticism. By actively addressing concerns, Starbucks leaders have converted some of their most ardent critics. Newspaper reporter Stephanie Salter is one such former detractor who had a change of heart because of Starbucks social responsiveness.

In an article in the *Terre Haute Tribune-Star*, Stephanie reports that some of her most unkind comments were directed toward Starbucks, "From the time the giant Seattle coffee chain went public . . . I have made unmerciful fun of everything about it." She then continues:

"In the meantime, [something] occurred to . . . nudge me toward eating crow. . . . The company responded to workers rights advocates and began to offer 'Fair Trade Certified™' coffee. . . . In the big scheme of global commerce, this was a welcome . . . gesture of support for thousands of perpetually exploited coffee workers in third world nations. For those of us who try to monitor the route between the goods we buy and the human beings who produce them, such a gesture goes a long way into positive territory."

Successful leaders do not hide from difficult challenges. They approach complex and controversial issues with a willingness to benefit from the concerns raised by commentators and adversaries. In the end, they take the course of action that not only quells criticism, but on occasion actually turns critics into company champions.

Fairly or unfairly, corporate criticism can emerge from factors outside of the business's control, posing unique challenges for leadership as it charts a way through tension and reticence. As an icon of American business, Starbucks has been met with significant resistance from those who fear globalization or who harbor negative sentiments about U.S. foreign policy.

As noted at brandchannel.com, author John Simmons believes that American companies should study how Starbucks has effectively turned around negative perceptions worldwide. From John's perspective, Starbucks demonstrates that

> As long as the core product stays true to its quality and principles, other elements of the offer can adapt to local market needs. Go to a Starbucks in China, Japan, France, Greece or Kuwait and you will drink the same espresso, but the food will have a local flavor. . . . Certain aspects of the brand are sacrosanct—no smoking even in smoking cultures, the adherence to the "third place" even where space is at a premium (Japan, for example). But where adaptation is needed to fit cultures, Starbucks adapts.

The adaptability that John refers to is a reflection of the effort Starbucks leaders invest in understanding how their product must merge into a particular community and not resist local influences. John goes on to demonstrate that management's encouragement of the *be involved* concept works to subtly break down the fear and resistance that is often experienced in other parts of the world.

John indicates that Starbucks executives rely on district and store managers to make strong connections with their communities throughout the world: "Encouraging contact with communities feeds back into the brand, diluting the sense that corporate America is rolling its tanks into town." As businesses grow or enter new markets, there needs to be a sensitivity to the initial fear that new communities may have about the company's expansion. It is through this sensitivity and a willingness to listen that most resistance yields.

"Corporate America rolling its tanks into town" aptly captures the perception that led to difficulty for Starbucks in its first effort in China. Starbucks entered the Chinese market in a respectfully small way, with a two-table cafe in Beijing's Forbidden City, but its mere presence was met with strong opposition in the press. These were the same media that for decades supported isolationism and anti-American political rhetoric. They promoted the words of Chairman Mao Tsetung in the 1950s when he described the United States as the "leader of the forces of global imperialism . . . the most dangerous enemy of the people of the world." As a result, it was no surprise when one newspaper likened Starbucks presence in China to a slap in the face of 1.2 billion Chinese citizens. Just two months into its operation in Beijing, local officials considered revoking Starbucks one-year business license.

Rather than panicking, Starbucks leadership listened to local officials and continued to adjust to the needs of Chinese consumers and their communities. Starbucks management, for example, expanded the size of the stores in China to provide the space that customers desired and increasingly addressed other unique marketplace challenges, such as reconceptualizing the "to go" versus "to stay" service ratio. In the United States, approximately 80 percent of Starbucks drinks are ordered "to go," while in China the ratio is inverted, with 80 percent of drinks ordered to be consumed in the store. By better understanding the market and responding to the unique needs of the region, Starbucks is emerging in the minds of Chinese patrons as a destination restaurant and not just an American beverage provider.

According to *Seattle Times* reporter Monica Soto Ouchi, Starbucks apparently has turned the corner of acceptability in China and is now considered a prestigious brand. "With increasing exposure to Western brands, the young, trendy, and affluent began to view Starbucks—or xing bake (shin bah-KUH) as it's called here—as a brand that signified success, status, and wealth. In China, Starbucks customers tend to walk down the street with their coffee cups, round green logo facing out." By understanding and addressing the concerns of the specific market, Starbucks leadership ultimately was able to create a brand message that was more meaningful for China's unique retail culture.

Never settling for past success, Starbucks executives continue to be vigilant about the needs of the Chinese market, while remaining responsive to the lessons learned from the resistance. The leadership, for example, looked for more ways to encourage community engagement and support, even when the company was viewed skeptically. Starbucks managers quickly identified the importance of education in Chinese culture. Accordingly, Starbucks executives committed $5 million to support educational efforts in China. Starbucks dedication to helping this market flourish was in turn praised by actor Ziyi Zhang, a star of the movie *Crouching Tiger, Hidden Dragon*, named one of the world's 100 most influential people in 2005 by *Time* magazine.

Instead of being viewed as a slap in the face of her fellow Chinese countrymen, Ziyi Zhang noted, "Upon learning about Starbucks decision to support education initiatives in China, I was moved. As a Chinese national, I am deeply grateful to global companies such as Starbucks for their philanthropy. I applaud them and support them and am always eager to be an advocate for caring that is borderless."

The lesson of Starbucks success in China is twofold: not only must businesses make the products and services they offer more meaningful to new markets, but they must understand what is important to individuals in those markets and demonstrate that they have a legitimate concern for individuals' well-being.

Never Try to Beat Them; Always Join Them

Resistance to a company or a product is often the direct result of a lack of information about the company or its product or service. Starbucks partners initially had some difficulty penetrating the Japanese market because they were trying to bring a coffee culture into an ancient tea society. As reported by Ginny Parker of the Associated Press, a competing coffee chain owner, Thomas Neir, noted that coffee drinkers in Asian cultures often "spent five minutes stirring Nescafé into hot water, and that was coffee. Very few people even knew that it came from a bean."

Starbucks executives knew that Japan offered a great opportunity, even though tea was the favored beverage. Coffee consumption in Japan was more established than many had assumed. Therefore, the challenge of the Japanese market involved elevating the quality preference of the consumer, an obstacle that Starbucks leadership had successfully overcome in the United States.

Ginny continues, "There is a deeply embedded coffee culture in this country. . . . Canned-coffee vending machines are everywhere, and people flock regularly to tiny cafés for coffee breaks while smoking or reading."

To be successful, Starbucks had to distinguish the quality of its coffee from what the Japanese consumer had previously experienced. Management did this, in large measure, by educating Japanese coffee drinkers on the difference between canned or instant coffee and aromatic, gourmet varieties.

Starbucks leadership explained the basic distinctions in coffee quality, from the species of bean to the four fundamentals of a great cup of coffee (proportion, grind, water, and freshness). This educational approach reverberated in a culture that highly values information.

In essence, leadership set out to teach consumers important distinctions between the coffee that was routinely available and the improved quality that Starbucks could offer. Through education, Starbucks leadership took initial market resistance, born from a lack of exposure to gourmet coffee, and turned it into a booming, sophisticated Japanese coffee market.

In fact, Ginny Parker reports that the world's busiest Starbucks is "not in Seattle, San Francisco, or New York. It's smack in the middle of Tokyo. The American coffee chain is finding that Asia is a vast, thirsty, and untapped market. From Beijing to Bangkok, it is converting tea-lovers into fans of Frappuccino® and other frothy coffee drinks." Ginny noted that in a short span of time, Starbucks leadership secured 250 stores in 10 key Asian markets. Through a continued focus on educating people in response to resistance, the number of Starbucks stores is now over 500 in Japan alone.

While Asian markets required education to overcome resistance, Starbucks faced a very sophisticated coffee consumer upon opening stores in France. Odilia d'Aramon-Guepín, director of Marketing in France, notes, "Starbucks offered a new and different coffee experience. Our customers were perhaps not aware of the concept of ordering and paying before enjoying their beverages, or even to giving their first name to the barista taking their orders. But with time, French patrons have embraced this special human connection and frequently comment on what a nice touch it is to have that personal interaction with baristas, which is so unique to us at Starbucks."

To gain acceptance, Starbucks leadership provided foods to meet local tastes, adding typical French pastries including croissants, pains au chocolat, and pains aux raisins. All these food items are organic and produced by local bakers. Odilia adds, "We know that an ever increasing number of local French customers are embracing the Starbucks Experience in Paris. The excellent coffee, friendly service, and the unique third place environment attract more and more new customers every time we open a store. We have been truly overwhelmed at how local communities around our stores are quickly making the Starbucks Experience part of their daily ritual." Frank Boosman, strategic marketing consultant and blogger, puts it well, "While I enjoy traditional Parisian café culture, I know that I can get skim milk with my Starbucks coffee. I know they'll be able to make almost any drink as a decaf. I know no one will be smoking in the café. So yes, I'd visit Starbucks in Paris."

It is obvious that business leaders must be culturally sensitive when conducting business abroad, but that same sensitivity is needed domestically as well. Because of the amazing diversity found within this country, some communities may have unique requirements that are quite different from those of neighborhoods only a few miles away.

Such is the case for district manager Amy Tingler, who shares her experience working in a location that has very specific needs. "We have two stores located in the Squirrel Hill area of Pittsburgh, which is a highly populated Jewish community," she explains. "As a company, we have developed products like our whole bean coffee and certain other coffees that are kosher. At the store level in Squirrel Hill, however, we started to get input that we needed to make some changes to create a Starbucks Experience that was more in sync with that community. For example, we received comments from our regular customers about the Christmas music we had been playing overhead. We took that input seriously and made changes in the music."

To address the concerns of this specialized market, Kristena Hart, a district manager who formerly was responsible for the Squirrel Hill stores, added, "We enlisted the help of a local rabbi, who identified which of our products were kosher. We then labeled those products accordingly. In essence, we took what the community wanted and translated it into action."

Not only did Starbucks leadership listen and partner with the rabbi, but in-store partners showed their sensitivity as well. Kristena noted, "Our partners understand that they need to serve their community and respond to its values and its priorities. Sometimes national campaigns that come from the Starbucks corporate office don't necessarily serve the needs of Squirrel Hill. When this is the case, our partners change the way products are presented in our stores. A great example of this occurred when partners received holiday baskets from Corporate with green and red ribbons attached. The partners at Squirrel Hill took the ribbons off and replaced them with blue and silver ones. In a small way, these actions softened the experience, said thank you, and showed community spirit."

Squirrel Hill demonstrates the value of flexible policies for companies of all sizes. This adaptability makes a company nimble enough to serve the needs of diverse market groups. Thus, leaders can look for ways to help their people lessen resistance and proactively incorporate the unique character and needs of a community.

Adopting this flexible posture can be a difficult and frustrating challenge for many businesses. As a result, corporate executives often deal only with criticism or push back in a reactive manner. Often small issues are ignored until the negative rhetoric takes on a life of its own. At that point, the business leader has very little choice but to address the concern, which is likely to have grown into a much larger problem. Leadership at Starbucks not only attempts to react to criticism early, but, where possible, anticipates potential areas of resistance.

This proactive approach is reflected in the Emerging Issues Council. This standing committee of senior officers at Starbucks meets regularly to anticipate and track potential problem areas, look for solutions, and gain consensus on acceptable courses of action.

Sandra Taylor, senior vice president of Corporate Social Responsibility, comments,

This council brings in dissenting voices among our senior leadership and helps us look to areas of our business that may experience complex future challenges. We come together and talk about varying points of view. We have done this for many issues, like efforts to more actively engage cocoa producers in West Africa. It's a very effective way for people to get their issues heard and to achieve buy-in for difficult decisions and policies.

Managers need to look forward for any and all potential obstacles, while monitoring problems that have plagued the company in the past. From the Starbucks leadership perspective, embracing resistance means not only responding to the forces that are coming up from behind, but also looking to the future, both for solutions and for other potential problems or areas of conflict.

We Don't Want You Here

As you've seen in Principle 1, "Make It Your Own," Starbucks management encourages partners to *be welcoming*. Normally Starbucks also finds itself to be a welcome addition in the communities it enters. Marion, Indiana, Mayor Wayne Seybold stated, "A lot of people look at a prospective town to see if there are businesses in that town which they are used to seeing, such as Starbucks. These individuals judge communities based on which national retailers are there. For that reason and many others, Starbucks makes a community stronger, and as such they were very welcome in Marion."

In a few instances, however, Starbucks has received anything but a welcome mat. Rather than packing it in or ignoring the concerns of citizens in the community, Starbucks leadership engages in active listening and responds to the community's issues.

District manager Shelli Taylor shares how she approached community resistance in a particular town in New Mexico. "There was a small café in town. It was really popular, an important part of the community, with an owner who was well respected. Even before we went there, people were telling us this town might not work for us, especially because the influential café owner was opposed to Starbucks. There was a perception that we would be taking over. It was the kind of pushback we get from being the Big Green Giant.

"Given the community's concerns," Shelli recalls, "a colleague and I went door-to-door to every single café in town and introduced ourselves. We listened and talked to people about their fears and affirmed our commitment to create a win/win for their businesses and for us. We acknowledged that certainly there would be competition, but we were more interested in adding value to the business environment. I must admit this was very scary, going into people's businesses when you sensed you might not be welcome. But it was important to do because it helped open professional and business relationships."

Shelli and Starbucks leaders in general realize that fear is often the emotion that fuels the greatest resistance to growing companies. Surrounding or existing business owners fear that the newcomer will shrink their piece of the pie. Often, Starbucks management has overcome these concerns by listening to people's issues and pointing out how the company has actually helped community businesses in thousands of neighborhoods around the country.

Shelli's interaction with the community resulted in a more positive perception of Starbucks, and ultimately proved decisive in the town's willingness to welcome Starbucks to the neighborhood. "It really helped when we stopped being a brand and instead showed up as people," explains Shelli. "We could then discuss the benefits of creating employment and how our presence strengthened the choices and reasons for customers to visit that section of town. If you're a restaurant, you don't want to be the only restaurant on the street. It's not good for business. If two or three more restaurants come in, hopefully different types, synergy forms, and people start to know they have options. Customers become aware of that restaurant-rich area, and a dining culture grows. People then develop habits, and the community of restaurants does well. It's no different for the coffee culture."

Shelli was ultimately pleased to share: "We had anticipated the owner of the nearby café would oppose us, but she was quoted on the local news saying, 'I own stock in Starbucks, and I think this is great for our town. I welcome them here.'" Clearly the efforts of Shelli and her colleagues paid off.

What if every business took the time to engage in conversation with those who are likely to create barriers? Rather than ignoring detractors or resisting them, these business leaders could be far more effective if they searched for common ground that could lead to successful partnerships.

While the media often dramatize the struggle between small coffee shops and Starbucks, fueling fears with banner headlines that imply a David-versus-Goliath-type battle, Starbucks actually creates an opportunity for smaller businesses to make their operations stronger. In an article in the *Fredericksburg (Virginia) Free Lance-Star*, Mike Ferguson, marketing communications director for the Specialty Coffee Association of America, notes that early on, "people opening coffeehouses were passionate about coffee, but weren't necessarily businesspeople. They had issues with competing. Today, they've . . . become businesspeople."

Mike provides an example from an area near his office in Long Beach, California, where there are "two Starbucks, another regional chain coffee shop, and two independent coffeehouses. They're all thriving, and one independent's business actually shot up 40 percent after the Starbucks stores opened because [the business owner] focused . . . on inventory control and teaching his staff salesmanship."

The *Free Lance-Star* article continues with Mike stating that Starbucks enjoys "34 to 37 percent of the market. . . . Independents stay steady at 51 percent. No matter how many stores Starbucks opens, the independents keep pace. It's like consumers almost need that option of having the independents [there]."

Ultimately, when other coffee shop owners resist Starbucks, they are often avoiding the changes they need to make in order to remain competitive. Starbucks leadership recognizes this resistance and, instead of using it as an opportunity to squelch competition, cooperates with those business owners to create a healthier and more vibrant marketplace. While new competition is almost always feared, in truth it can infuse energy into existing businesses. Competition can require a company to reevaluate itself—identify its strengths, address its shortcomings, adapt, and improve.

There are times, however, when resistance is powerful. It may require far more than the personal visits made by Shelli Taylor in New Mexico. Sometimes leaders have to find ways to connect with the core of a community before resistance will yield. Leeann Mesa, Ventura, California, district manager, discussed anxieties that were raised when Starbucks was opening its first store in the city of San Fernando, a predominantly Hispanic community.

As Leeann explains, "There were similar coffee shops in the city of San Fernando, and nobody really wanted us to go there. There was a lot of resistance from some members of the city council, but also from the community." Leeann grew up in the San Fernando Valley. "It was really important for me to give back to the community. I wanted to embrace its very artistic nature." Upon opening the store, Leeann contacted a local artist. "I asked him if he'd be willing to bring some of his artwork into my location. He was more than happy to do so. So, for a three-month period, we took down Starbucks artwork and placed his amazing murals on our walls. We had such an overwhelming response. People appreciated that we would involve someone from their community."

Leeann continues, "Later we had an art exhibit, and Starbucks created postcards that we sent out to the community and handed out in our store. The proceeds of the event went to a youth organization that educated future mariachi musi-

131

cians. We had close to 300 people show up at this small drive-through Starbucks, and the mayor also attended. It was just such an incredible experience."

For Leeann, softening the relationship between Starbucks and the San Fernando community meant "opening up forms of communication and paying attention to the input of our customers. For example, our menu was mostly in English, and we had to make a transition. At the beginning it was difficult. We were able to receive some informational pamphlets in Spanish that helped us advertise our product a little better. But it was literally the partners who came from the community and spoke Spanish who helped customers appreciate our offerings."

Leeann and her team found ways to turn initial cautiousness into a motivator for growth. Leeann puts it best:

Once people in the community were able to get past the Starbucks "corporation," they saw that we were intimate with our customers. We're one-on-one, personable, and approachable. I think that's the key word: approachable. When you say "embrace resistance," that's what I think of—being approachable. Not that we will fix everything for you, but that we will stay open to you as you share your needs and reactions with us.

While most resistance can be overcome with patience and concerted effort, there are times when resistance is simply too strong. The leadership challenge in these situations is accepting that the resistance needs to be honored. There comes a time in business life when resistance actually increases in proportion to the efforts to defuse it. This is an indication that the best move is simply to walk away.

Starbucks leadership has experienced situations in which excessive resistance has been encountered when entering a market. District manager Renny Freet shares one of those encounters: "We had an issue in Long Beach, California," explains Renny. "We had a presence in the area, with seven stores. Since Long Beach is a large metropolitan region, seven stores aren't that significant. We found a location in the Long Beach area called Seal Beach. It was a former Burger King restaurant that had been vacated."

From the onset, the Seal Beach location met with intense community resistance. Renny shares, "We'd go to council meetings and listen to citizens who saw us as a threat to local independent coffee shops. Several of those coffee shops were actually chains themselves. Some of the competitors were able to get articles in local newspapers saying less than flattering things about us and suggesting that we were a nuisance. It was difficult for me to read those articles, and frankly they were untrue."

Rather than attempting a media blitz that would counter the resistance, Renny claims, "We just did what we do. We became increasingly involved in the community. We organized activities that served Seal Beach from our other Long Beach locations."

This story, however, does *not* conclude with a warm embrace from the neighborhood. As Renny puts it, "We ended up not going after the location we had been pursuing because we felt the timing was wrong." But instead of blaming the community for the resistance, Renny concludes, "We knew we hadn't done as good a job as we could have at involving ourselves in that community. But we've built stores in the area since, and the opposition wasn't anything like we experienced in the past. Embracing resistance is a lot about respecting other people's perspectives. When the resistance doesn't ebb, it's time to choose to take the high road and say there will be other sites on other days." Becoming involved in the community (even when it is wary of you), patiently waiting for greater acceptance, and on occasion deciding to table the opportunity for a better time, all represent the discipline that distinguishes great organizations from impatient, myopic ones.

Whether in the community or in their stores, Starbucks leaders have learned that walking away from short-term battles often promotes a healthier, more collaborative long-term future. Former store manager Gerald Kyle (now a district manager) experienced this firsthand. He comments, "The customers at the Pike Place Market store came in expecting to find the same pastry product line they could find at any other Starbucks. However, our lease agreement is fairly restrictive at that historic location. For example, we were not allowed to sell fresh food and could sell only boxed or packaged food items. Over the months, customers kept asking for more food options. So, we started wrapping pastries and selling them to meet customers' demands. Some of the other vendors in the market apparently complained and said we were in violation of our lease by selling those wrapped pastries."

Gerald prepared an argument for market officials, in the hope that he could persuade them to allow him to continue to sell food. The crux of his argument was that many of the people who complained were also violating their leases by selling espresso. Before Gerald made his pitch, however, he spoke with his district manager, who gave him valuable insights into why it was important for him to honor the terms of the lease in response to the concerns raised by other vendors.

As Gerald explains, "I remember my district manager looking at me and saying, 'Gerald, we're Starbucks, and we just have to be bigger than all of that.' He was correct. In this case, the right thing was to not get petty." Starbucks scaled back its food offerings at the original store and accepted the resistance of the neighboring merchants. In so doing, the company's leaders validated the importance of blending into the community while resisting the urge to push through with their own corporate desires. At times, great leadership is little more than making sound compromises.

Beware the Naysayers

One of the most challenging types of resistance faced by every business is that from those who say, "It can't be done." Many individuals are quick to suggest that your ideas are not sound or that they will cause your business to suffer. Rather than believe the skeptics, the leadership at Starbucks seems to ask the question, "Why *wouldn't* it work?"

If the answer Starbucks receives in response to that question is a compelling one, such as that a particular product is too far afield from the company's core business or that the idea compromises quality, then the leadership will accept the reasonable boundary and move on. However, if it is simply a matter of "It hasn't been tried before," Starbucks executives look for a way to explore the viability of the option. For example, when Starbucks leadership began considering musical products, cynics derided the idea with statements like, "Music may not be Starbucks cup of coffee," or this may "prove to be another ill-fated attempt to sell something else, anything else, with the Starbucks name on it."

Starbucks executives pressed on, cautiously testing how music and the Starbucks Experience fit together. The leadership didn't simply give up on the idea, but instead examined how music meshed with core business objectives. Ken Lombard, president of Starbucks Entertainment, comments, "Music turned out to be a pretty natural fit. It's been part of the Starbucks environment and culture from the very beginning. From the early days, we were among the first retailers to use music to set the mood in our stores."

Rather than simply accepting doomsday prognostications, Ken looked to Starbucks customers to determine the wisdom of venturing into the music industry and music sales. "This is something our customers gave us permission to go beyond. Thousands of times we'd have customers coming in, hearing something playing overhead, and asking the barista, 'What's the name of that song? Where can I get it?' So there was a connectivity that was really more us offering our customers what they were asking for than trying to put something in the store that they felt we were trying to sell to them. Combine that with how often our customers are in our stores. What we're trying to do is provide them with quality music options, give them a special opportunity to discover music beyond limited formats, and do all that as part of their daily routine."

Starbucks management honors only one limit when it comes to selling music: the sale can't interfere with the customer's in-store experience. Everything else can be worked through. As Ken notes, "That's what Starbucks has been about from the beginning. It's being innovative, it's being entrepreneurial, being positioned to take advantage of opportunities that we feel first and foremost add value to the Starbucks Experience.

"We would never come in and abuse what we're doing in the existing stores, or compromise the integrity of the coffee experience. That is sacred to us—it will always be sacred to us. But music gives Starbucks an opportunity to add value and enhance the customer's experience instead of taking away from it." The key, when responding to negative business predictions, is a willingness to examine how any new venture fits naturally and meaningfully into your current business model. In other words, be open to innovation as long as that idea is true to the original mission of your company.

The Starbucks brand has come a long way with the music business in the last decade or so. It has been a persistent journey from its 1995 collaboration with Blue Note Records, when it produced an initial compilation CD. Mileposts along the way have included the 2004 Grammy Award®–winning album with Ray Charles and successful relationships with Herbie Hancock, Elton John, the Rolling Stones, and many other musical forces. Starbucks now is a springboard for the careers of new artists like Antigone Rising and Sonya Kitchell.

The positive media coverage that Starbucks has garnered in recent years is evidence of how far it has come in refuting its critics. In an article published at www.foxnews.com, columnist Michael Y. Park wrote, "What may be the most powerful name in music doesn't belong to a record label, a powerful industry executive, or an influential band. In fact, it doesn't belong to a company associated with music at all. . . . Starbucks Coffee may be the future of music in America." Nothing soothes the sting of criticism as much as success that disproves the skeptics.

The world is filled with people who will tell you that you and your business will fail. While critics can be helpful in identifying potential stumbling blocks, their doomsday forecasts are little more than opinions (and often ill-informed ones at that). Successful business leaders figure out how to determine whether the sky is falling or the sky is the limit. Ultimately, by focusing on values, objectives, and feedback that can make them better, great companies exceed the expectations of customers, employees, and the communities they serve.

When Customers Say No

When you are faced with customers who thumb their noses at your company's product or service, there are two viable options: either experiment with new ideas that might turn customers around, or abandon the product altogether. When green tea Frappuccino® blended beverage, a popular product in the Pacific Rim, was first introduced into Western markets like Canada and the United States, customers resisted. Nancy Poznoff, a product manager for Starbucks, states, "We tested green tea Frappuccino® blended beverage in Richmond, British Columbia, a suburb of Vancouver. Richmond is a high Asian density market. We had positive results among the Asian population, but non-Asians weren't gravitating to the product."

The challenge for Starbucks leadership was to find a solution that appealed to new customers, while not alienating the original market. As Nancy reports, "This product is a really good example of just how passionate people in this company are. It also shows how important our people are to the success of a product. Teams at Starbucks came together to brainstorm how to help this product appeal to all of our customers. How could we easily customize green tea to meet the needs of Asian customers who've been drinking matcha (precious top-grade, hand-picked Japanese gyokuro green tea) in their tea ceremonies since they were babies, as well as those who have never experienced green tea?

"After considerable effort, we didn't just develop one flavor, but instead created a delivery system for cooking the tea, so that we could make it from matcha tea powder, which was traditional for Asian tea drinkers, and then pump in a melon syrup, which appealed more to Western palates. If someone didn't want the sweetness or didn't want the melon flavor, they could skip it and just get closer to that original international product. With all that work in product development, we took the two types of green tea into testing and we found that we had hit the nail on the head on the first try. It was highly unlikely, but we made it happen."

While Starbucks leaders' first thought may have been to plunge directly into the Western market with green tea products, they instead listened to customers in that market to learn more about their preferences. Because Starbucks took the appropriate steps to address its customers' concerns ahead of time, green tea Frappuccino® blended crème and green tea latte had a hugely successful introduction.

No matter how convinced we may be about the probable success of a product or service, we are often too close to our own ideas to objectively evaluate their viability. When confronted with red flags, many managers either ignore the warnings or convince themselves that the warnings are wrong. Successful leaders understand that careful evaluation of resistance often makes the difference between success and failure.

While some products can be changed to catch customers' fancy, others can't be modified to live up to their initial promise. Rather than continuing to present these resisted products to the consumer, there comes a time to reconsider the offering. This is something I have experienced personally. My son, daughter, and I were visiting a Starbucks in my hometown when we noticed a sign for "Chocofino." It was offered as a sipping chocolate. Fortunately for us, the store was giving out samples and asking for our reactions. My daughter and I thought it was heaven-sent, while my son thought it was too rich and sweet.

Little did I know that our market was a test site for a product that was later rolled out as Chantico™ drinking chocolate. I enjoyed the drink and even liked the improved name (Chantico is the Aztec goddess of the home and the domestic hearth). I felt that Starbucks had made another brilliant decision to offer a delicious product that could attract people into its stores in the evening hours.

Despite a seemingly excellent product breakthrough, however, Chantico™ drinking chocolate did not capture the passion of enough Starbucks customers, and ultimately the product was discontinued.

Instead of viewing the introduction of this beverage as a mistake, however, Starbucks, in its classic style, saw it as a learning opportunity. In its formal communication announcing the discontinuance of Chantico™ drinking chocolate, Starbucks indicated, "We don't see [Chantico™ drinking chocolate] as a failure. We see it as an opportunity to leverage what we've learned from our customers to provide chocolate beverages that we're going to be excited about." With the end of Chantico™ drinking chocolate came the announcement that Starbucks would be offering two new chocolate drinks. It is the rare business leader that knows how to leverage setbacks and losses into future gains.

Errant Perceptions and Taking Valid Responsibility

In a world in which information moves globally at the speed of light, misinformation can become a monumental source of resistance for businesses. Even when swift counteraction is taken to set the record straight, one can never be certain how many people were contaminated by rumors and false information.

The Starbucks brand has occasionally borne the brunt of such negative and false information. In 2004, when troops were deployed in both Iraq and Afghanistan, Marine Sergeant Howard Wright apparently heard a story from a friend, who had heard it from yet another person. That story prompted Sergeant Wright to fire off the following e-mail:

"Please pass this along to anyone you know. This needs to get out in the open. Recently Marines over in Iraq supporting this country . . . wrote to Starbucks because they wanted to let them know how much they liked their coffee and try to score some free coffee grounds. Starbucks wrote back telling the Marines thanks for their support in their business, but that they don't support the war and anyone in it and that they won't send them the coffee. . . . We should not [buy] any Starbucks products."

Of course there was *no* such policy in existence at Starbucks, and there was no evidence in support of that wild claim. At the time, the Starbucks leadership reaffirmed the company policy:

"Starbucks has the deepest respect and admiration for U.S. military personnel. We are extremely grateful to the men and women who serve stateside or overseas. We sincerely appreciate that they are willing to risk their lives to protect Americans and our values of freedom and democracy. While Starbucks as a company cannot directly donate to military personnel, many of our partners show their support by donating coffee."

141

Although it's nearly impossible to act quickly enough in a world of instant messaging and mass e-mailings, Starbucks leadership swiftly addressed the misinformation in Sergeant Wright's e-mail in hopes of averting lasting damage to the brand. Ultimately, Starbucks efforts led to a retraction e-mail from Sergeant Wright. In it he stated,

"Almost 5 months ago I sent an e-mail to you. . . . I heard by word of mouth about how Starbucks said they didn't support the war and all. I was having enough of that kind of talk and didn't do my research properly like I should have. This is not true. Starbucks supports the men and women in uniform. . . . So I apologize for this quick and wrong letter I sent out to you. Now I ask that you all pass this e-mail around to everyone you passed the last one to."

The reputation of a business or brand can be seriously affected by rumors, half-truths, and misinformation. Before errant information gains momentum, leaders urgently need to find ways to communicate the whole truth to set the record straight.

On the flip side, in order for a business to maintain the trust and credibility of its key constituencies, senior managers must be willing to take full and immediate responsibility when errors do occur.

On September 11, 2001, Midwood Ambulance Service employees responded to the terrorist attack on the World Trade Center in New York City. Shortly afterward, an e-mail surfaced, which reported,

"My family owns an ambulance service in Brooklyn, NY. . . . My uncles were at 'Ground Zero' during the attack, to help the victims. They donated their time to help with this crisis, as many New Yorkers did. A great number of people were in shock from the devastation. As many of you know, shock victims are supposed to drink a lot of water. My uncle went to the Starbucks down the street to get bottles of water for the victims he was treating. Can you believe they actually charged him for it! He paid the $130 for three cases of bottled water out of his own pocket. Now, I would think that in a crisis such as this, vendors in the area would be more than happy to lend a little help by donating water."

The e-mail continued, "I love Frappuccinos® as much as anyone, but any company that would try to make a profit off of a crisis like this doesn't deserve the . . . public's hard-earned money. Please forward this e-mail to anyone you know and encourage them to do the same."

Unfortunately, this e-mail was accurate. A Starbucks partner had chosen to charge full price and not give away $130 worth of water during the September 11, 2001, tragedy. In addition, several efforts to get the matter resolved were mishandled. When the e-mail surfaced, Starbucks leadership did the right thing. Then president and CEO Orin Smith not only had a $130 check delivered to the ambulance company, but he called a representative of the business personally to apologize. Independently, the Starbucks stores located at Ground Zero were operating around the clock and they were providing free beverages and pastries to rescue workers and volunteers.

At a corporate level, Starbucks was making contributions in excess of a million dollars to the national relief fund. But the bad news of the water sale certainly made a big splash in the pool of public consciousness. Starbucks leadership fortunately understood that most people are willing to forgive human error. What they won't tolerate is a failure to take

143

responsibility for mistakes or an unwillingness to resolve the shortcoming.

With the grace of competent leadership, Starbucks did not seek to scapegoat or place blame on the store partner who made the errant decision in an unimaginably stressful situation. Instead, Orin Smith understood something that most great leaders appreciate: when you are wrong, admit it, fix the problem, and stay the course in areas where you are making a positive difference.

Resistance inside the Store

For a company to be truly successful at embracing resistance, individuals at all levels must be empowered to deal in a proactive manner when things run amok. At Starbucks, in-store partners emulate the behavior of their leaders. Since they have the most face-to-face interactions with customers, partners must be well trained in how to deal with unhappy and resistant patrons.

Store manager Holly Vanderknapp describes what happens when her staff confronts the prospect of turning down a customer request. "We have a 'just say yes' policy. When a customer asks for something, we explore how we can make the request into a reality for the customer."

"Unfortunately," says Holly, "there are times when we can't say yes, particularly if it involves the safety or health of someone else. Whenever possible, we try to work with customers and their special needs. For example, we have a lady who requested an odd drink alteration. The first time she came in, she ordered 15 pumps of chai, 2 pumps of cinnamon, with nonfat milk poured into a cup, and then she wanted it steamed all together. That's not something we normally do. The partner said that he could do everything but steam the syrup with the milk. He knew that doing that could clog up the steamer. Rather than telling the customer that it couldn't be done, he let her know that we would look into it for the future. In the meantime, I called someone in charge of maintenance on our machine, and he advised that it would not be a problem. We looked for an option, rather than saying no, and we found one."

Holly notes that her team frequently thinks in terms of alternatives: "For whatever reason, sometimes people bring their own milk to add to their drink. Our baristas let them know that because of health concerns, we can't steam their milk in our steamer. But the partners always offer a suggestion that will work, such as putting the espresso in one of our cups and then having them add their milk so that it can be shaken as an iced beverage." Here, finding a solution means simply explaining store policies and mixing in an innovation or two.

Business today is complex. While many things may appear black and white, growing a business or leading a team often requires a willingness to think in shades of gray. In fact, progressive business leaders ask themselves and encourage their employees to ask not "yes or no," but "how." They set stretch goals and encourage themselves and their colleagues to achieve more than they thought was possible.

Taking it one step further, Starbucks leadership helps partners look for nonverbal cues to customer resistance, even if the customers haven't shared their dissatisfaction directly with the partner. According to district manager Lisa Lenahan, "There's an art to knowing if your customers are displeased. You can read their body language, and you should be able to take care of concerns before you are even asked.

Don't wait until customers come to you and say they're really upset—if they're tapping their foot or crossing their arms, you should already know that something is not quite right.

"Sometimes we encourage customers to try something new," says Lisa. "If we're paying attention, we will look over and notice if they seem to be enjoying the new item. If the customer seems dissatisfied, we'll offer to trade out the new food or beverage for what the customer usually orders. Partners feel very comfortable doing that, especially if they know they're making a person's day. It's a small gesture, but it can really turn somebody around. When you have an experience like that in the store, when somebody takes the time to notice that you weren't enjoying something and they take care of it before you have a chance to complain, it is an amazing experience."

Few businesses actually react constructively to obvious resistance, let alone encourage their people to look for subtle and less obvious signs of tension. But for a company to be truly successful, workers at all levels must become attuned not only to what their customers *are* saying, but equally to what they *aren't*.

People take note when a company receives and responds to feedback constructively. Customer Leslie Alter observed an interaction between another customer and a barista: "The other day, a woman came into Starbucks. Her baby was with her. When she came out of the rest room, she seemed upset and told one of the baristas, 'You really ought to have a changing table in there. I'm sure there are a lot of women who come in here with their children.' The barista responded, 'That's a great idea; thank you for sharing that with me. I will mention your suggestion to our manager so he can take action on it.' The lady definitely seemed satisfied with the response. The way the barista calmed her down was very effective."

Beyond calming the customer down, the barista reportedly advised her manager of the need, and the situation was swiftly remedied. Similarly, partner Rick Mace adds,

> *I remember being so impressed with one of the managers at the Pike Place Market store where I worked. Her name was Allison, and she had a remarkable ability to listen to customers' complaints and do something about them. In fact, there was this woman who used to walk or bike a good distance to come to our store. She would frequently come in and complain, "There is no place for my coat." Allison listened and, on her own, went out and bought a little coat hook. Allison put it by the door with a big bow, and it's still there today. In fact, when customers ask for a tour of the original store, it's one of the things I am quick to point out.*

Why let complaints go ignored when you can use what others are saying to enhance your business and the overall customer experience? The ability to act positively on any criticism is a crucial leadership skill. When leaders listen to complaints, it not only helps customers, but models the behavior that the leaders hope to see in the people who work for them and with them.

Unfortunately, efforts to address customer concerns sometimes lead to new forms of resistance. District manager Gerald Kyle notes, "One day Pork & Beans, an enormous fiberglass pig, bigger than four or five people, was delivered to the Pike Place Market store. Pork & Beans is actually covered in dark roasted coffee beans from hoof to snout; hence, the 'beans' in her name. She was designed by artist Sandy Nelson, a partner from our creative group, when Starbucks commissioned artists to produce three pigs in support of a fund-raiser. Unfortunately, Pork & Beans interfered with traffic flow, and we began to hear complaints from customers."

While trying to address the customers' needs, Gerald ran into a new series of difficulties. "We couldn't put her outside because the weather would destroy her, so I decided we could probably mount her over the front door. That really created roadblocks, as we were limited in the structural changes we could make in the store. My team had to get the permission of the Pike Place Market Historical Commission and ultimately work with store designers to draw plans for how Pork & Beans was to sit above the door. The staff had to demonstrate how the sow was going to be supported, how she was going to be earthquake-proofed, and how she wasn't going to affect the historical impression of the store."

"The longer Pork & Beans sat near the counter, the more complaints we received," continued Gerald. "The more we tried to solve the dilemma, the more resistance there was from the historical commission. With perseverance, though, we were able to get approval, partner with the maintenance guys from the Pike Place Market, and move Pork & Beans to her perch above the door. And there she sits, oblivious to all the work she caused."

Even with all its open-minded policies and never-ending leadership quest to do things better, there are times when Starbucks partners can't solve a problem. While persistence enabled them to move a pig, Starbucks executives couldn't do much to stop elephants and other migratory animals from tramping through a coffee estate near the Ngorongoro Crater in Tanzania. So Starbucks leadership and the estate had to just accept the paths determined by the animals. When resistance beats you, all that is left is your creative spirit. Playfully, Starbucks named a premier coffee from Tanzania, from its

Black Apron Exclusives™ line, Elephant Kinjia. (The name *kinjia* comes from the Swahili word for "path.")

While the path of an elephant may not be easily diverted, most other forms of resistance can be resolved through active listening and a commitment to use feedback for long-term growth. Great leaders drop the defensiveness and open their ears and minds to the input of others, accepting resistance as a valuable developmental tool.

Create Your Own Experience

- How willing are you and your business leaders to listen to the criticisms of others?

- How seriously do you take problems, and how early do you bring in your critics for problem solving?

- When do you avoid people because of the fear that interactions with them will be unpleasant or conflictual?

- Think about how often you say no at work. In what situations could you have created a possible yes, or at least a maybe?

Ideas to Sip On

Nothing in nature grows without facing limiting forces.

- Embracing resistance involves a complex set of skills that enable businesses and individuals to create business and relationship opportunities when they are confronted with criticism, skepticism, irritation, or wariness.

- To work with resistance effectively, you must distinguish between people who want their concerns to be resolved and those who simply like to complain.

- While it's natural to avoid contact with detractors, much can be gained by welcoming them into the early stages of problem-focused discussions.

- When the concerns of critics are allayed, those critics can often become your most ardent supporters.

- It is essential to correct misinformation swiftly.

- When errors are made, it is important to take direct, unequivocal responsibility and follow up with corrective action.

- Embrace resistance—unless, of course, there are elephants involved.

leave your mark

"How wonderful it is that nobody need wait a single moment before starting to improve the world."

—ANNE FRANK

All of us leave some mark on the world. What varies is whether that mark is positive or negative. Do we give back more than we take, or do we take more than we give? This is particularly important in the world of business, where the actions of managers have a profound effect on individuals and society. Some leaders are content with hitting the firm's profit goals. They cut corners on everything from employee benefits to capital expenses. Others, however, believe that an important part of their business success is linked to the powerful and positive impact that they have on their communities.

Social involvement is integral to Starbucks leadership mission, and therefore community participation serves to export the Starbucks Experience to people around the globe. Starbucks executives have a monumental commitment to corporate and community stewardship that includes taking care of their own staff, volunteerism within neighborhoods, quality-of-living considerations for product providers, economic transparency through the supply chain, large grants to national community organizations, seed grants for local nonprofits, planned sustainability for future generations, and environmental preservation efforts. And that's only part of Starbucks socially active approach.

So why would a company's leadership invest so much time and effort on social concerns? Do Starbucks managers give so much back to their staff and to their communities because they think that it's the right thing to do or because it attracts more business? Even if leaders initially decide to be good corporate citizens because they hope it will boost profits, almost all who sustain that type of commitment do so because it becomes the best way—the only way—to do business. From my time spent exploring all levels of the

Starbucks organization, I've concluded that this company is the real deal.

Starbucks leadership captures the company's social commitment in the mission statement, which notes that Starbucks will "contribute positively to our communities and our environment." Beyond simply stating that commitment, managers at Starbucks work diligently to make sure that their mission and values guide their day-to-day business decisions. In fact, Starbucks leadership has even developed a separate mission statement that captures the company's specific commitment to environmental concerns. It states,

Starbucks is committed to a role of environmental leadership in all facets of our business. We fulfill this mission by commitment to

- *Understanding of environmental issues and sharing information with our partners*

- *Developing innovative and flexible solutions to bring about change*

- *Striving to buy, sell and use environmentally friendly products*

- *Recognizing that fiscal responsibility is essential to our environmental future*

- *Instilling environmental responsibility as a corporate value*

- *Measuring and monitoring the progress of each project*

- *Encouraging all partners to share in our mission*

153

Starbucks values-driven approach requires coordination among various parts of the business to oversee and implement socially responsible practices. The Starbucks board of directors, the company's CEO and president, and The Starbucks Foundation—a separate 501(c)(3) organization—all work in concert with the senior vice president of Corporate Social Responsibility to guide policy and to guide the implementation of these community-oriented priorities. Various departments, such as Business Practices and Corporate Social Responsibility, are designed to bring Starbucks community objectives into reality. This department not only focuses on current social programs, but also looks for new ways to reach out to the communities with which Starbucks is involved. As Sue Mecklenburg, vice president of this group, suggests, "I've seen Corporate Social Responsibility move from being a matter of philanthropy to being the way we run our business. It's transformational!"

Many managers, nevertheless, may feel that they don't have the same resources to devote to community-based programs, especially when compared to a large organization like Starbucks. In truth, the size of a company only partly explains the magnitude of its social impact. The scale of any leadership's conscience and the size of its heart also play a big role. Small and midsized companies can do amazing things for the people who work for them and for their neighbors. They can make a big splash in a smaller pond.

Unfortunately, leaders in companies of all sizes, from mom-and-pop stores to multinational conglomerates, often fail to realize what they can do to contribute to their communities and to society as a whole. Starbucks leadership represents a powerful exemplar of ways to be a success at business while being a life-enhancing force for individuals and communities.

The View from 30,000 Feet

The topic of corporate social responsibility (CSR) has been buzzing around the business world for more than a decade. Of course, during this period, we have seen many corporate executives being taken away in handcuffs to answer a dizzying array of charges, including insider trading, fraud, and embezzlement. In the United States alone, about half of all adults are skeptical of big business and question the truthfulness and ethical behavior of most companies and their leaders.

If for no other reason than to allay consumer wariness, leaders are well advised to lift their eyes from the bottom line and consider their communities. Businesses that thrive today are led by managers who understand the importance of investing in their people (beyond a competitive salary) and in their neighborhoods (both proactively and responsively). Multiple research studies have found that

155

- People prefer to do business with and work for socially conscious companies.

- The most talented and qualified applicants are increasingly considering a company's ethics and community support when selecting their employer.

- Employee morale is three times higher in firms that are actively involved in the community than in their less-involved counterparts.

- When employees' work environments match their personal values, they are more productive.

- Companies that focus on environmental impact typically are valued up to 5 percent higher than comparable organizations without that focus.

- The participation of employees in community-based activities strengthens their teamwork, leadership skills, and corporate identity.

Most leaders would be happy to see the benefits just listed reflected in their annual report. However, the effects of social responsibility are extremely difficult to quantify and articulate. Over the years, business executives have even struggled to identify what it means to be socially responsible. Sometimes the definition is so narrow that it is reduced to fundraising efforts in the community. Other times it is so broad that it sounds like a beauty pageant contestant who, when asked for her primary goal in life, answers "world peace."

Steve Priest, founder of the ethics and compliance consulting firm Ethical Leadership Group, offers a very accessible definition of "leaving a mark." In an article for *Global Finance*, Steve shares,

> *A company is socially responsible if it takes seriously its obligations to all of its stakeholders. It's not about whether a company sponsors local events or environmental programs, or has a foundation that gives money to charitable causes. It's about developing a reputation of integrity so there is trust with employees, investors, customers, suppliers, and their communities.*

Socially committed business leaders, like those at Starbucks, depend on the trust that they earn when the company successfully fulfills its obligations.

Building Trust

The value of the Starbucks brand is 100 percent linked to the trust that stakeholders place in the company. Starbucks is given permission by a broad universe of people to conduct business robustly, as long as those people feel that the leaders do what they say they will do. Starbucks management has been successful in evoking trust from stakeholders by caring for employees, delivering to customers, providing a quality product, enriching investors, and improving communities in a way that helps the environment.

Given these broadly defined accomplishments and ongoing objectives, people who have an interest in Starbucks measure the company's performance relative to its own priorities via a concept referred to as the "triple bottom line." This measurement requires Starbucks leadership to report not just financial results, but also its social impact and environmental performance. These findings are published in an annual, independently audited Corporate Social Responsibility (CSR) report, which is easily accessible in its entirety directly from the company or on its Web site, and in an abbreviated version in Starbucks stores.

By taking a strong stand on social issues and holding itself publicly accountable for delivering on its commitments, Starbucks has attracted the interest of many different constituencies, not least of which are top job applicants. Sheeba Oriko, one such candidate, became a Starbucks partner in the IT department.

Sheeba states, "Prior to working for Starbucks, I'd worked with many different global companies. Each was very successful, but I'd never heard of a company having a social conscience. That intrigued me. I dug a little bit further and found out that Starbucks was committed not only to social responsibility, but to setting the direction for and leading the corporate social responsibility movement. It took me about a year and a half of networking to get a position at Starbucks. During that time, I kept researching the company and meeting Starbucks partners. The more I explored the company, the more I was attracted to what they stood for and to their goals."

Sheeba, who is originally from East Africa, has been a strong addition to Starbucks. Given her experience with drinking water problems in her native land, Sheeba brought to Starbucks not only her IT knowledge, but also a passion for, and a rare understanding of, the impact of global water issues on women and children worldwide. Sheeba has used her knowledge to work with Starbucks to support water projects through its Ethos™ water brand.

Talented individuals like Sheeba are frequently attracted to socially responsible companies because they know that such companies offer both challenge and fulfillment. Most of us want to be involved in organizations that care about more than financial success. Yet, before you race into your manager's office to promote socially responsible programs, understand that even the most ardent proponents of CSR concede that the financial advantages of this approach are difficult to measure, see, or experience in the short term. CSR is not a fad to be tried until a new one comes along. It is a paradigm shift in the way business gets done, and it can prove to be a long, bumpy, albeit hugely rewarding, ride. With commitment over the long term, substantial gains are realized through community involvement. Patient leaders produce impressive benefits for their organization and for the broader social world.

A Triple Shot of Socially Responsible Business Practices

Throughout this book, there have been dozens of examples of how Starbucks senior managers looked past the bottom line in opening stores, harvesting coffee, and conducting business. These leadership actions—including employee benefits decisions, C.A.F.E. Practices policies, development of relationships with environmentally conscious and socially diverse companies, and community involvement—have been addressed in earlier discussion. It's important to see how these commitments help Starbucks leave its mark in communities throughout the globe.

Benefits for Partners

When Howard Schultz and senior management made the decision to offer health-care benefits to all employees who work 20 hours a week or more, they were going beyond the call of duty. A strong business case could have been made that such benefits were not necessary. Other quick-service restaurants did not provide that level of health-care coverage. Entry-level jobs in this sector are typically minimum-wage positions without any health-care benefits. While retention problems plagued the fast-food industry, many analysts believed that Starbucks did not need to go as far as it did to hold on to employees.

Indirectly, the company's decision to offer health-care coverage to "part-timers" put pressure on other companies to provide similar compensation packages or deal with the consequences. Some communities object to big retail superstores invading their neighborhoods on the basis that their effect is to *lower* the salaries of employees in existing businesses. By contrast, communities often appreciate Starbucks because its arrival in a neighborhood usually *raises* the expectations for other similar employers.

C.A.F.E. Practices

As was noted previously, Starbucks has developed an evolving set of guidelines for buying coffee. If coffee suppliers meet certain criteria, they can negotiate a long-term, premium price for the coffee they sell to Starbucks. However, if a supplier wants to be a stable provider for Starbucks, it must commit to being independently measured on these criteria, which include

- Opening up its books so that Starbucks can see how it pays its providers, all the way down to the coffee picker

- Working with Starbucks to develop environmentally friendly practices, such as decreased pesticide use and lower water consumption

- Constantly improving the living conditions for its laborers

- And, of course, maintaining a high level of product quality

Starbucks generally pays a higher price for its coffee than its rivals pay (approximately $1.26 more per pound), and a Starbucks supplier contract, under C.A.F.E. Practices guidelines, guarantees a premium price that will protect the farmer from the volatility of the coffee market. This helps providers plan their coffee businesses more strategically—buying land, investing in equipment, increasing salaries to workers, and securing loans.

Does Starbucks have to pay a premium fixed rate instead of paying the lowest price possible for acceptable-quality coffee? Does it have to give incentives so that its suppliers focus on the environment and on better social conditions for their workers? As a matter of practicality, it doesn't. But Starbucks has chosen to go beyond being just a coffee purchaser. Leadership focuses instead on the relationships with those in the supply chain, banking on the idea that if you improve the future for those who support you, your future will be secured as well.

Partnerships with Environmentally Conscious and Socially Diverse Companies

For better or for worse, we are, at least in part, affected by the reputation and behavior of our colleagues and the organizations for which we work. Unfortunately, we all know that there are companies that hire suppliers based only on price, with no concern for the suppliers' business practices—using sweatshop subcontractors, for example. By contrast, from Starbucks leadership's perspective, social responsibility requires an assessment of the values and corporate diversity of the people who sell to the company.

Each year, Starbucks sets high standards for attracting a diverse base of contractors and product providers. For example, Starbucks seeks to increase the percentage of suppliers who are more than 51 percent women- or minority-owned. Similarly, Starbucks has forged business partnerships with firms like Johnson Development Corporation, founded by Earvin "Magic" Johnson, or acquired businesses, like Ethos Water, that have demonstrated compatible diversity support or environmental concern.

The innovative business partnership between Starbucks and Johnson Development Corporation is called Urban Coffee Opportunities (UCO). UCO is a 50/50 joint venture that

161

was formed in February 1998 to provide employment opportunities, training, and quality products in economically disadvantaged metropolitan communities. UCO integrated the retail strength of Starbucks with Johnson Development Corporation's expertise in stimulating opportunities in urban areas.

Ken Lombard, who was formerly president and a partner in Johnson Development and is now president of Starbucks Entertainment, reflects: "That was absolutely on the cutting edge of companies going into minority communities with a solid commitment to doing the right thing and providing people who live in those communities with the same quality options that people in the suburbs have. Howard Schultz was very enthusiastic about it; the company embraced it. And despite skepticism from some, it turned out to be a great example for retailers and other operators like Starbucks. We went into minority communities, demonstrated profitability, and built a significant business."

Business partnerships like Urban Coffee Opportunities work because they empower people to overcome adversity, prejudice, and other negative social influences. With a sound business model, the creation of opportunity, and a belief in human potential, leaders encourage their people to strive for and achieve greatness.

Giving Back: Writing Checks and Igniting Service

Community service groups and community-based organizations often need both money and volunteers to achieve their mission and realize their goals effectively. Fortunately, every one of us has the ability to affect, if not secure, both corporate giving and community volunteerism. Starbucks leadership has created support for communities throughout the world by developing The Starbucks Foundation and by creating ways to encourage corporate volunteerism. The Starbucks brand, in turn, has benefited from this, achieving strengthened bonds in the neighborhoods the company serves, increased pride among its partners, and an exemplary reputation for philanthropy and community service.

Corporate Giving

As businesses grow, they often face the perception that "big" equals "bad." Many people assume, for example, that large companies lose their heart and their compassion. To ensure that Starbucks maintain a focus on stewardship during its growth, Howard Schultz established The Starbucks Foundation in 1997. This foundation centralized Starbucks corporate giving efforts and prioritized support for literacy and programs affecting children and families.

163

While the magnitude of Starbucks financial giving is impressive, at the end of the day, it is the impact of those dollars that really matters to the people whose lives are affected. For community partner Jumpstart, it has meant more than a decade of literacy education and progress toward the goal that every child in America will one day enter school prepared to succeed. In 2005, The Starbucks Foundation pledged $1.5 million to Jumpstart alone. This money is intended to support the organization's efforts over the next three years.

While $1.5 million is outside the budget of most philanthropists, most of The Starbucks Foundation grants fall between $10,000 and $50,000, and all of those dollars go to organizations in which Starbucks partners have volunteered. Once partners have worked with an agency and have witnessed that agency's positive impact on the community, the organization can apply for support from The Starbucks Foundation.

One organization that has benefited greatly from The Starbucks Foundation and the volunteer work of Starbucks partners is DeafHope, a community group that provides services to deaf domestic abuse victims. Julie Rems-Smario, executive director of DeafHope, says, "The employees of Starbucks are our angels—they have been so generous with their time and talents to improve the DeafHope house by remodeling and improving our wiring system to meet the demands of technology and accessibility."

It was through the involvement of Starbucks partners that DeafHope secured a $25,000 grant from The Starbucks Foundation. Julie shares that with the Starbucks grant, Deaf-Hope is able to continue to provide free support services for survivors, upholding its mission to end domestic and sexual violence against deaf women and children through empowerment and education.

What does DeafHope's mission mean in the lives of those it serves? Julie reports that a mother of four told her, "I left my abusive husband who was starting to hurt my children too. I had no place to go. The shelters were not accessible. The police could not understand me. My children and I needed safety, and we found it at DeafHope."

Donna Cahill, executive director of Holy Family Day Home, an organization providing early educational child care, summarizes the impact of Starbucks corporate giving. After her organization received a $50,000 grant from The Starbucks Foundation, Donna simply noted, "Thanks. . . . You really are serving more than coffee in our community."

For Starbucks leaders, serving communities often takes them off the traditional path of Fortune 500 companies. Sandra Taylor, senior vice president of Corporate Social Responsibility, observes, "We have one effort with our Tazo division and with Mercy Corps, where we are supporting projects in 24 villages in Darjeeling, India, a tea-farming area. One project is to improve water and sanitation. Through efforts thus far, the residents of the region have seen a 10 percent reduction in waterborne diseases. That's huge for a coffee and tea company!"

Sandra goes on to explain that the Darjeeling project also offers vocational training to tea-farming families. "One thing about tea farms is that there is only one child who gets to carry on the family business. So whether you're an owner or a worker, there are children who have no employment within tea, and in many cases no employment at all. We are helping young men in the area learn skills like electronic equipment repair. One young man asked, 'Why would a coffee company care about us and what we do?' I think a better question would be, 'Why wouldn't we?' They are part of our community."

Just how big is *your* "community"? Great leaders not only grow their businesses, but in the process tend to expand their concept of community. For Starbucks leadership, social responsibility reflects a very broad sense of community. In Singapore, Starbucks is leaving its mark by opening a store that serves as a training arena for students' work and life skills. The store, called the Pathlight Café, is the first of its kind in Singapore. Eight autistic adolescents between the ages of 12 and 15 are being trained in the skills necessary to handle money, serve customers, and make sandwiches. Denise Phua, acting principal of the school, views Starbucks generosity as integral to the students' developing "good skills, attitude, and work habits that will make them competent for future employment."

In nearby Malaysia, Starbucks leaders opened the Berjaya Starbucks Coffee and HOPE Worldwide Penang's Free Pediatric Clinic. The clinic provides medical services at no cost to individuals who don't have the financial means to get pediatric care. To keep administrative costs down, Starbucks partners in Malaysia volunteer at the clinic and assist with the administrative work, maintenance, and medication preparation. Partners have also conducted fund-raisers for the clinic and organized presentations for families that visit the clinics. If that isn't enough, the Starbucks partners in Malaysia also collect books and used clothes from all over the country to donate to the children served at the Free Pediatric Clinic.

Pragmatists might question why Starbucks leadership facilitates the training of autistic adolescents or the delivery of medical service. In both cases, the company addresses the needs of individuals who may never be Starbucks customers. Starbucks leadership, however, believes not only that it is right to support these endeavors, but that, in turn, these civic efforts forge stronger alliances between Starbucks and local citizens, politicians, and community leaders. Starbucks gains acceptance as a true and compassionate member of these communities, not just a foreign interest entity that is out to make profits for the people back home.

Community Volunteerism

By encouraging employees to be volunteers, business leaders can have a tangible, low-cost, and immediate impact on their neighborhoods. Starbucks executives support volunteerism on many levels, including the "Make Your Mark" program. Consistent with *be involved,* one of the Five Ways of Being outlined in Principle 1, Starbucks challenges its staff members to make their individual mark right where they live. In support of this, Starbucks makes a $10 per hour contribution, up to $1,000 per project, to the qualifying organization where the partner volunteers.

Lara Wyss, a Starbucks partner in the media relations department, affirms, "For every hour I am in my school reading to my daughter's class, Starbucks is making a cash contribution to the school. They aren't paying me to volunteer. They are enhancing the impact of my volunteerism in my community." An added benefit of such programs is that employees feel that their company truly cares about what they care about, and, in turn, they feel more loyal to the company and more engaged in their work.

As Starbucks executive Sandra Taylor suggests,

Often people think that corporate social responsibility means that you have to have a lot of money and that you have to be prepared to give a lot of money to the community. But when people ask me how to get started as a community steward, I tell them they need to think about mobilizing their people as volunteers. If a group of employees decide to clean up their street or park, that's engaging in the community, and that's a real exhibition of how much they care, as opposed to the company just handing out cash. For us, it's proof that you can do good and do well at the same time.

Grandview Elementary School in Vancouver, Canada, knows the good that can come from the involvement of Starbucks partners. Grandview is an inner-city school that nearly closed in the mid-1990s as a result of increased violence in and around the school. In the late 1990s, Starbucks partners began to tutor students. This once-failing school is now a national success story. In 2001, only 22 percent of fourth-grade students were reading at their grade level; in 2004, that score quadrupled to 88 percent!

Wendy Fouks, literacy specialist at Grandview, says, "The impact the Starbucks partners had as tutors in the lives of these kids is priceless. Their consistent, caring presence made the difference for our children. Ironically, I think our kids may have made a difference for the volunteers, as well." Wendy gives an example of the rewards experienced by a particular Starbucks volunteer. "Adrienn was from Europe and had a bit of an accent. When she first came here, she seemed concerned that she might not be effective at reading with our kids. But as she went along, she gained confidence in her ability to communicate effectively with the children. I think it gave her and all of the volunteers a sense that they were contributing and making a difference for the future lives of the children."

While many can volunteer, Wendy suggests that few have assumed the level of responsibility shown by the Starbucks partners. "Starbucks staff were reliable. Volunteerism is a part of their culture—their identity, if you will. You could count on them to be there when you expected them. It has been an amazing relationship."

Not only does this type of volunteer involvement show people in a community that you care about them, but it also gives employees the opportunity to get to know one another better—both inside and outside the company. Paul Boardman, district manager in the Vancouver region and one of the volunteers in Wendy's program, shares, "Most businesspeople are busy, but these volunteer contributions are important. I find in my stores that our partners feel great about contributing. Sometimes we just need to give our people the opportunity and let it go."

In addition to their volunteerism, these partners encouraged Grandview to apply for a grant from The Starbucks Foundation. The school received its first grant in 1999 and a second grant in 2004. Caroline Krause, former principal at Grandview, conveys, "Quite frankly, without the support of Starbucks and others, we would not have a reading program. We were in dire straits. We really didn't even have the money to be able to purchase the books we needed."

Volunteers like Paul and Adrienn and others in Vancouver not only learn new skills and contribute to their community, but also take satisfaction in their contributions and have fun. To the benefit of Starbucks, volunteerism strengthens team identity and enhances leadership abilities.

Store manager Janeen Simmons offers an example of how team building occurred during a Seattle-based project: "Partners from a number of different downtown districts in the Seattle area made a small local park our volunteer Earth Day project. We were going to pour cement, build a big arbor, and do a couple of other projects. What a sense of team and community we developed that day among partners who might not have been able to be together in any other context. Everyone was there—baristas, shift supervisors, managers, district managers, our regional director, and even our regional vice president." By modeling volunteerism at the leadership level, partners throughout the organization understand that community involvement is a prized value in the Starbucks culture.

Volunteerism in any organization generally doesn't happen by chance. It usually requires someone to take the responsibility for identifying appropriate needs and organizing events. Starbucks leadership has put a system in place to ensure that partners actively seek ways to reach out to their neighborhoods. As Starbucks executive Sandra Taylor explains, "We call the partner who spots opportunities a 'community lead.' In every district, there's a store manager who's very engaged in the community on behalf of the district. They're identifying possible community programs in which the district can engage."

Starbucks district manager Renny Freet describes one activity in his community that has become an annual tradition. "Each year we go down to the post office, and we get all the Santa letters. We read through the letters, and we choose the most challenging ones, like, 'My father is out of a job and we have no Christmas.' We then fulfill the requests made in the letters! Around Christmas Eve, we go out as a group and deliver the presents. If the person in the letter wants a bicycle or a bed or anything like that, we deliver it."

Renny says that as an added benefit, this volunteer activity has created connections in the region. "What's great is how it has spread out from Starbucks to other local businesses. Those businesses often make large donations of items, and we get to partner with them in building a community of giving. If only you could see the eyes of those who receive the gifts. We are businesses, sure, but we are people who want more from our lives than just doing a job. We want to give something special to people. We can, and do, offer ourselves on behalf of others."

Volunteerism also helps employees set ambitious goals and develop the management skills to realize those goals. The components necessary to achieve success in volunteer initiatives are frequently the same as those required of leaders in business projects. Team goal setting, strategic thinking, progress charting, and course correction abilities can all be developed and enhanced in a volunteer setting—to the indirect benefit of the workplace.

District manager Karen Mahoney saw this type of leadership development when her team worked with Habitat for Humanity. Karen relates, "I enjoyed watching the partners set a lofty fund-raising goal and exceed it through hard work. It was also gratifying to see something they were so passionate about. Once the building phase begins, we will be volunteering weekly as a team to build a home for some needy family. Each Saturday during the construction, we'll also contribute coffee and bring it to the site in the morning to get everybody started. This whole thing came from our partners, and they are excited to see their dream, a house for a needy family, about to be realized."

Future Leadership

Although Starbucks leadership has already left a huge mark on communities throughout the globe, the company isn't finished yet. If anything, the management at Starbucks has started to appreciate the unique opportunity available at this point in the company's history. Managers are aware that they may change more than local communities and that they have a role in sharing the lessons they have learned from their CSR journey to date.

Sandra Taylor sums it up well: "Up to now, in Starbucks history, we've committed to doing the right thing. We've conducted our business in ways that reflect our values and our principles because we thought it was good for our partners and our suppliers, but only in recent years have we talked about how we can be an example for leaders of other industries. We aren't arrogant enough to say 'follow our lead,' 'we're the best,' or anything like that, but we've had success and we've had validation for the way we've conducted our business. We believe we can offer insights for others to model."

As for leadership in specific areas of social responsibility, Sandra adds, "On health care, we are talking about how we are able to provide for our partners and why we think that's a good model for industry. We also want to offer our coffee-purchasing guidelines to other coffee companies as a guide to having sustainability in their relationships with coffee farmers. And we're looking to see if those buying principles can be applied to the purchase of other agricultural commodities, like cocoa, dairy products, and pulp for paper. It might lead to a universal way to achieve sustainable agriculture. All of this not only allows our partners to serve quality coffee and create uplifting experiences, but actually helps them be a positive force for change in their world and—dare I say it—gives them a chance to improve the world at large."

172

Starbucks partners can make a difference on a large scale, as witnessed by their actions following the massive tsunami that struck southern Asia in 2005. In the immediate aftermath of the tsunami, Starbucks in-store partners in Phuket, Thailand, gave thousands of baht (the local currency) of their own money to the community to buy food, water, and cloth to wrap victims' bodies. The leadership in Thailand supported their efforts by having Starbucks stores in Thailand proclaim a "Day of Giving," during which 100 percent of store profits were designated for relief. Globally, Starbucks donated sizably to tsunami relief efforts and offered customers opportunities to do so as well.

Through a commitment to social responsibility, Starbucks leadership has opened possibilities for partners so that they can have a more tangible impact on the broader world. By guiding their staff members to think and act in ways that contribute to their neighborhoods and important social causes, these leaders help employees realize their power to make a difference. Such a realization encourages us all to be what Mahatma Gandhi suggested we could be, namely, "The change we wish to see in the world."

Create Your Own Experience

- Can you find ways for you and your business to leave the biggest, most powerful mark possible?

- Will it be volunteerism, fund-raising, community grants, or a more overarching commitment to examining the impact of your business practices?

- How do you think these efforts would benefit your community (added volunteer resources, completion of projects that could not have occurred without your company's assistance, or some other way)?

- In what ways might corporate social responsibility help your business?

- In what ways can you use community outreach to build teams and increase employee engagement?

- What are you waiting for?

173

Ideas to Sip On

Successful business leaders realize that a key part of their success is leaving a powerful and positive mark on their communities.

- Many business executives initially decide to be good corporate citizens because they hope it will improve their business, but almost all who sustain that type of commitment do so because it becomes the right way— the only way—to do business.

- People want to do business with, work for, and invest in socially conscious companies.

- Employee morale is three times higher in companies where community involvement is an integral part of the business model than in their less-involved counterparts.

- By participating in community-based activities, employees are given the chance to build their leadership skills and grow as teams.

- The value of a business's brand is 100 percent linked to the trust people place in the company to do what it says it will do.

- Corporate social responsibility shouldn't be seen as a passing fad. Instead, it should be valued as the way global business gets done.

- You can be the change you wish to see in the world!

a final word

Congratulations! Your Experience Awaits

It is no accident that you picked up this book. At some point, you must have asked yourself, "What can I learn from a company like Starbucks?" You took the time to explore the principles that made the company such a success. Starbucks reflects an empowering and entrepreneurial work culture, fosters consistent customer loyalty, amply rewards faithful shareholders, and offers an opportunity to make a difference in the world.

You probably have already begun to think about ways in which you can extract ideas from this book and apply them to your own business or life experience. You may even have thought about how you can gain buy-in from other leaders in your organization so that the members of your staff truly "make your business their own." You might have thought about instilling corporate guidelines that give your people an image of what it would look like to *be*, not just *do*, the things that matter most to your business.

For Starbucks leadership, the framework—*be welcoming, be genuine, be considerate, be knowledgeable,* and *be involved*—is critical to creating the Starbucks Experience for partners, suppliers, customers, community groups, and everyone who comes in contact with the company.

While these *ways of being* are critical for Starbucks, you will probably need to tailor them to your own business and industry. For example, if you run a hospital, you might add "be compassionate," or a high-tech firm might wish to emphasize "be innovative."

In any case, your guiding tenets need to offer a flexible structure so that you can implement those values while fostering the special gifts and passions of your people. Just as leaders at Starbucks help their partners understand that *be welcoming* means "offer everyone a sense of belonging," you will need to operationally define what your "ways of being" will generally look like.

Howard Schultz looks to his own experiences to help partners understand what it means to live the Five Ways of Being. In an interview with *Context* magazine, Howard reflected on a positive and unexpected experience that he had after a sushi dinner in Tokyo. After the meal, Howard went to thank the 70-year-old restaurant owner for both his skill in preparing the sushi and the overall quality of the experience, but the proprietor couldn't be found. Howard notes, "It turned out that [the owner] was waiting out on the street on a cold night, holding the door to my car open. He didn't just finish the meal by bringing us a cup of coffee, as most places do. He finished the meal by putting me in my car and thanking me for coming to his restaurant."

While being interviewed on a popular morning television program the next day, Howard was less interested in talking about Starbucks than about telling the story of his dining experience and mentioning the name of the restaurant. For Howard, the emotional connection he felt as a customer at that sushi restaurant was equivalent to what he wants partners to do on a daily basis. Howard went on to ask, "Do we do it with everyone? No. But that is the intent. We try to enhance people's days and make them feel good about being

176

at Starbucks. That, for me, captures what business should be about."

Much like Starbucks, you may wish to support and enliven your core business concepts with examples from your experience, ongoing dialogue, internal communications, customer feedback, and training that demonstrates when your team *is being* and when it *is not being* that which is valued by your organization.

You may choose to implement Starbucks ideals in your business by addressing the details that often get overlooked in the rapid pace of your business day. Rather than accepting shortcuts and subpar efforts, you may choose to challenge your team or workplace to adopt an Everything Matters approach.

Starting with a vision of what your business would be if it were truly operating at its best, you and your team can expose the roadblocks that keep it from consistently performing at an optimal level. These factors, which are the difference between ordinary and extraordinary, may surface in the customer satisfaction, product quality, training, or social involvement aspects of your organization.

177

By embracing both the feedback and resistance of customers, community groups, and staff, you will be given ample opportunities to observe the details that mean the difference between getting by and creating exceptional success. To that end, you may wish to examine how you and your business deal with dissent and criticism. You may think about ways, as does Starbucks leadership, to go beyond responding to complaints and actually anticipate them. You will probably find opportunities to bring dissenters into problem-solving discussions and create structures in your business that track emerging concerns.

Starbucks is an excellent model of how a company can become a learning institution. Starbucks leaders understand the importance of taking feedback, both positive and negative, and disseminating it throughout the company for collective education and adaptation.

You may want to jump right to the "surprise and delight" aspects of your business, immediately discovering ways to maintain a consistent, predictable, and comforting experience for internal and external customers. You may examine breakdowns in product or service consistency and solicit input on the "felt sense" that people have about you and your company. You might work with your teams to discuss ways to playfully delight one another or to add a "prize" when serving others.

Finally, why not champion a broader sense of social involvement for your business? You will be offering your people a chance not only to grow your company, but to grow their communities and their personal legacy in the process. You will expose ways to build your team while serving others outside the physical confines of your business.

So where should you start? It is typically best to begin in areas that are in concert with your passions and that are likely to offer immediate gains. But when it comes to your journey with the Starbucks Experience, *where* you start matters less than *when*. What matters is that you take action now.

Strike While the Coffee Company Ideas Are Hot

Often we get inspired by the ideas or practices of others, but we fail to put those ideas into operation. Given that tendency, I offer the following plan of attack for taking the Starbucks Experience and unleashing its potential for your business today.

Consider doing a personal inventory of how you stack up against the Starbucks Experience principles. Consider the following questions:

- How consistently welcoming am I?

- What details do I tend to overlook?

- Where can I offer more surprise or delight in my workplace?

- In what situations do I embrace resistance, and when do I run from it?

- What mark am I leaving at work, at home, and in my community?

Discuss the Starbucks Experience principles with a like-minded person or your work team.

Where possible, encourage all team members to look at your collective performance in relation to these principles. For example, in corporate assessment and strategic planning sessions, ask these questions:

- As a team, what are your strengths with regard to accepting criticism, executing the details, or delighting customers?

- What are your weaknesses when it comes to balancing your profitability with your broader mission?

- How can you help encourage greater product and service innovation throughout your business?

From this evaluation and planning exercise, great things can happen! As anthropologist Margaret Mead so eloquently

179

stated, "Never doubt that a small group of thoughtful, committed citizens can change the world. Indeed, it's the only thing that ever has."

Excellence versus Perfection

With all this talk about changing the world, I fear I may be leaving you with the impression that Starbucks is a near-perfect company. Such an impression could actually work against your putting these principles into action. Who wants to aspire to unattainable goals? In truth, Starbucks leaders have made their share of missteps, and store partners are subject to all human foibles.

While I have tried to stay on course with transferable lessons from Starbucks, I certainly have collected the occasional sad stories of partner conflicts, baristas who called in sick at the last moment, bad service moments, and even in-store romances gone bad. Overall, my experience as a customer at Starbucks has been very positive and uplifting. In fact, as I waited for a drink recently, I had a barista playfully apologize by saying, "I am sorry for your long wait, but we are taking great care to ensure that your drink is lovingly handcrafted by our indigenous baristas." I loved that.

Unfortunately, I've also had Starbucks visits where it was clear that my barista just wasn't with the program that day. But, on balance, Starbucks is an exemplary business—one, as I suggested in the introduction, that qualifies as a culture-changing growth story of our time. Starbucks excellence emerges from visionary management, a passionate entrepreneurial spirit, a social conscience, and guiding principles that are inculcated into the fabric of the business.

The Future: Starbucks and Your Own

It is difficult to imagine all the great things that are yet to come for Starbucks. Howard Schultz keeps suggesting that the company is in the "early stages of growth," "the second inning of a nine-inning game," and the "beginning chapters of a long book." As examples, Starbucks has announced plans for aggressive growth in China, in-store downloading of music on customers' MP3 players, espresso dating in conjunction with Yahoo!™ Personals, and the distribution of movies and books. But whatever its future holds, you can be assured that Starbucks will be well grounded in the Starbucks Experience principles that have been outlined herein.

What does the future hold for you and your business? Where might the Starbucks Experience principles take you? I suspect it may be a journey to the extraordinary.

bibliography

Introduction

"The Starbucks story epitomizes 'imagine that' in every sense. When the company went public . . . it had just 165 stores clustered around Seattle . . ."
—Cora Daniels, "Mr. Coffee: The Man behind the $4.75 Frappuccino Makes the 500," *Fortune*, April 14, 2003.

"Starbucks Corporation went public in June 1992. On the first day of trading, the stock closed at $21.50—up from an opening price of $17. Not only did . . ."
—Samuel Greengard, "Stock Options Have Their Ups and Downs," *Workforce Management*, vol. 78, no. 12 (1999), pp. 44–47.

"The way we have built our company by including the success of the company with everyone in it and not leaving . . ."
—Geoff Kirbyson, "Howard Schultz, Not Your Average Joe," Brandcareers—Profile, www.brandchannel.com, August 30, 2004.

"Starbucks employees have an 82% job-satisfaction rate, according to a Hewitt Associates Starbucks Partner View Survey. This compares . . ."
—Maryann Hammers, "Pleasing Employees, Pouring Profits: Caffeine Addicts Aren't the Only Fans of This Corporate Legend, Which Serves Up Warm Fuzzies with Its Cold Frappuccinos," *Workforce Management*, October 1, 2003.

"the leading retailer, roaster and brand of specialty coffee in the world" is part of the banner included on all Starbucks press releases.

"The success of Starbucks demonstrates the fact that we have built an emotional connection with our customers . . ."
—Kirbyson, "Howard Schultz"; quote edited slightly
   by Lara Wyss, Starbucks Media Relations.

". . . noticed, tucked deep in the corner, apparently not for customer inspection, a bulletin board. It was jammed with pictures . . ."
—Seth Godin, "Inside and Outside," http://sethgodin.
   typepad.com/seths_blog, July 20, 2005, paraphrased
   by the author for ease of readability in context.

"stay small while growing big"
—phrase coined by Howard Schultz in response
   to the challenge of growth; from Chris Gorley,
   Starbucks Global Brand Communications.

Principle 1: Make It Your Own

". . . truly encapsulates the core philosophies of Starbucks. Cover to cover, it may take five minutes to read . . . and that's if you pause . . ."
—David M. Martin, "The Bank Blitz Memo:
   Welcome to Coffee Talk," Tom Brown's
   bankstocks.com, www.bankstocks.com,
   November 29, 2005.

"Instead of overwhelming folks with reams of minutiae and too-rigid instructions, it gives guiding principles of the environments they hope to create . . ."
—Martin, Bank Blitz Memo.

"Remember that a person's name is to that person the sweetest and most important sound in any language."
—Dale Carnegie, *How to Win Friends and Influence People* (New York: Simon & Schuster,1964).

"We are not in the coffee business serving people, but in the people business serving coffee. The equity . . ."
—Howard Schultz interview, "The Art of Creating Passionate Consumers: Howard Schultz," *Know*™, Spring 2005.

Information about Starbucks replacing 5 percent of the energy used in its U.S. company-operated stores with wind energy and reducing its carbon dioxide emissions by 2 percent was obtained from an article by Kristen Millares Bolt, "Starbucks Taps into Wind Energy Production," *Seattle Post-Intelligencer*, April 15, 2005.

Information about contributions of $10 million to water projects in developing countries over the next five years as part of the acquisition of Ethos Water was obtained at www.ethoswater.com, March 2005.

"I just went down in my purse and I found enough change to include everybody. We . . ."
—Associated Press, "13 California Starbucks Workers Share $87 million Jackpot," CNN.com, October 25, 2000.

"We here at Starbucks work as a team and we support one another. And if I would have taken all the money, then I wouldn't have . . ."
—Natalie Allen, CNN Anchor and Lou Walters, CNN Anchor, "Starbucks Manager Mary Champaine Discusses Winning $87M California Lottery," *CNN Today*, aired October 25, 2000.

"People want to be part of something bigger than themselves. They want to be part of something that touches their hearts."
—Howard Schultz interview,
  "Creating Passionate Consumers."

Principle 2: Everything Matters

"Retail is detail"
—Phrase coined by Howard Schultz; from Chris Gorley,
  Starbucks Global Brand Communications.

"The Starbucks sensation is driven not just by the quality of its products but by the entire atmosphere surrounding the purchase of coffee . . ."
—"Starbucks: A Visual Cup o' Joe," @ *issue*, Corporate
  Design Foundation, vol. 1, no. 1.

"felt sense"
—Dr. Eugene Gendlin, *Experiencing and the Creation of
  Meaning* (New York: Free Press of Glencoe, 1962).

"Starbucks management looked upon each store as a billboard for the company and as a contributor to building the company's brand and image. Each detail . . ."
—Arthur A. Thompson, Jr., and A. J. (Lonnie) Strickland,
  Strategic Management Concepts and Cases, 11th ed.
  (New York: McGraw-Hill, 2003).

"After more than two years of testing and developing prototypes of this cup, the data did not clearly indicate that the final version . . ."
—Report of the Starbucks Coffee Company/Alliance for
  Environmental Innovation Joint Task Force, April 15,
  2000.

Information about using 10 percent recycled materials in beverage cups was obtained from a Starbucks press release, "Starbucks Demonstrates Its Commitment to Social Responsibility throughout Its Business in Fiscal 2005 Corporate Social Responsibility Annual Report," February 8, 2006.

Principle 3: Surprise and Delight

Information on Cracker Jack® was found at the Cracker Jack® Web site, www.crackerjack.com.

"As I pulled up to the store, I knew something was terribly wrong; the sign was still dark and the lights were off inside. I stopped the car and went . . ."
—Michael Cage, "Why Starbucks Wins & What Local Businesses Can Learn from Them," Marketing and Entrepreneurship, www.entrepreneurslife.com, June 14, 2005, paraphrased by the author for ease of readability in context.

"noncustomers"
—Peter F. Drucker, *The Essential Drucker: In One Volume the Best of Sixty Years of Peter Drucker's Essential Writings on Management* (New York: Harper Business, 2003).

Information about the surprise to Bernadette Robinson was found in the archives at www.oprah.com for November 30, 2004.

Principle 4: Embrace Resistance

"The trait of Starbucks that has appealed to me the most in the past has begun to weaken. That trait is consistency. Simply, I think it was once . . ."

—David M. Martin, "The Bank Blitz Memo: Wake Up and Smell the Latte," Tom Brown's bankstocks.com, www.bankstocks.com, April 18, 2005.

"One lesson I think we can all learn from this is that no brand is unassailable. I've heard scores of banks in the past mention Starbucks . . ."
—Martin, "Bank Blitz Memo: Wake Up."

"A few days after the column posted, I was in an airport, and picked up a voicemail message that caught my attention. The call was . . ."
—David M. Martin, "The Bank Blitz Memo: Welcome to Coffee Talk," Tom Brown's bankstocks.com, www.bankstocks.com, November 29, 2005.

"The entire experience reinforced a few lessons for me . . ."
—Martin, "Bank Blitz Memo: Coffee Talk."

"From the time the giant Seattle coffee chain went public . . ."
—Stephanie Salter, "Starbucks Order: One Latte and a Dish of Crow," *Terre Haute Tribune-Star*, April 30, 2005.

"As long as the core product stays true to its quality and principles, other elements of the offer can adapt . . ."
— John Simmons, "Starbucks: Supreme Bean," brandchannel.com, November 21, 2005.

"With increasing exposure to Western brands, the young, trendy, and affluent began to view Starbucks—or xing bake . . ."
—Monica Soto Souchi, "A U.S. Icon Counts on China to Fill Its Cup," *Seattle Times*, October 9, 2005.

"Upon learning about Starbucks' decision to support education initiatives in China, I was moved. As a Chinese national, I am deeply grateful . . ."
—Starbucks press release, "Starbucks Commits
   US $5 Million to Support Educational Programs
   in China," September 19, 2005.

"spent five minutes stirring Nescafé into hot water, and that was coffee. Very few people even knew that it came from a bean."
—Ginny Parker, Associated Press, "Starbucks Turning
   Asian Tea-Drinkers into Latte Lovers,"
   Reno Gazette-Journal, May 30, 2000.

"There is a deeply embedded coffee culture in this country. . . . Canned-coffee vending machines are everywhere, and people flock . . ."
—Parker, "Starbucks Turning Asian Tea-Drinkers."

". . .not in Seattle, San Francisco, or New York. It's smack in the middle of Tokyo. The American coffee chain . . ."
—Parker, "Starbucks Turning Asian Tea-Drinkers."

" . . . people opening coffeehouses were passionate about coffee, but weren't necessarily businesspeople. They had issues . . ."; "two Starbucks, another regional chain coffee shop, and two independent coffeehouses. They're all thriving, and one independent's business actually shot up 40 percent after the Starbucks stores opened because [the business owner] focused . . . on inventory control and teaching his staff salesmanship."; "34 to 37 percent of the market. . . . Independents stay steady at 51 percent. No matter how many stores Starbucks opens, the independents keep pace. It's like consumers almost need that option of having the independents [there]."

—Cathy Jett, "Coffee Clash: Mom-n-Pop, Starbucks, Go Head-to-Head," *Fredericksburg (Virginia) Free Lance-Star*, December 1, 2005.

"What may be the most powerful name in music doesn't belong to a record label, a powerful industry executive, or an influential . . ."
—Michael Y. Park, "I'll Take a Venti Latte . . . and a CD," www.foxnews.com, January 4, 2006.

"We don't see [Chantico] as a failure. We see it as an opportunity to leverage what we've learned from our customers to provide chocolate . . ."
—Information from Lara Wyss, Starbucks Media Relations.

"Please pass this along to anyone you know. This needs to get out in the open. Recently Marines over in Iraq supporting this . . ." and other related quotes
—"Starbucks and Iraq," TruthOrFiction.com, www.truthorfiction.com.

"My family owns an ambulance service in Brooklyn, NY. . . . My uncles were at 'Ground Zero' during the attack . . ."
—"Starbucks—Water at Ground Zero," TruthOrFiction.com, www.truthorfiction.com, and "Starbucks Apologizes for Water Flap," www.foxnews.com, September 26, 2001.

Information about the elephant pathways and Elephant Kinjia coffee was obtained from a Starbucks press release, "Coming Through: Elephant Kinjia Coffee Stampeded into Starbucks; Sixth Black Apron Exclusives Coffee Combines Exotic Flavor and Ingenious Farming Tactics," May 2, 2005.

Principle 5: Leave Your Mark

Information cited from research studies was obtained from many sources. Of particular note are Dan Keeler, "Spread the Love and Make It Pay," *Global Finance*, May 2002; Andrea D. McCombs, "Working to Make a Difference," *Savannah Morning News*, December 27, 1998; Alistair C. Ping, "Why Community Involvement Makes Good Business Sense," *Insight Works* www.insight-works.com, March 1996.

"A company is socially responsible if it takes seriously its obligations to all of its stakeholders . . ."
—Dan Keeler, "Spread the Love and Make It Pay,"
    Global Finance, May 2002.

Information about The Starbucks Foundation's pledge of $1.5 million to Jumpstart was obtained in a Starbucks press release, "Starbucks Renews Commitment to Literacy with $1.5 Million Donation to Jumpstart; Jumpstart and Starbucks Celebrate at Arizona State University Learning Festival," April 28, 2005.

"Thanks. . . . You really are serving more than coffee in our community."
—Full-page advertisement, *San Francisco Chronicle*,
    August 20, 2004.

". . . good skills, attitudes, and work habits that will make them competent for future employment."
—"Starbucks Opens New Shop in Singapore to Teach
    Autistic Children Skills," www.chinaview.cn,
    January 20, 2006.

Information about the Penang's Free Pediatric Clinic was obtained at www.Starbucks.com.my.

Information about the tsunami and the partners in Phuket, Thailand, was obtained from a Starbucks press release, "Starbucks Donates $100,000 to Southeast Asia Relief Efforts," December 29, 2004.

A Final Word

". . . It turned out that [the owner] was waiting out on the street on a cold night, holding the door to my car . . ."
—Interview with Howard Schultz, "Mr. Starbucks: Chairman Howard Schultz Says Building a Brand Now Is HarderThan Ever," *Context Magazine*, www.contextmag.com, August 2001.

". . . the second inning of a nine-inning game" and related quotes
—Andy Serwer and Kate Bonamici, "Hot Starbucks to Go," *Fortune*, January 26, 2004, as well as conversations with Lara Wyss, Starbucks Media Relations.

Much of the content of this book emerged from face-to-face meetings with Starbucks executives, including

Jennifer Ames-Karreman, director of Customer Service Operations/Customer Care Manager

Martin Coles, president, Starbucks Coffee International

Jim Donald, president and CEO

Dub Hay, senior vice president, Coffee and Global Procurement

Ken Lombard, senior vice president and president, Starbucks Entertainment

Carlos Maria Rodriquez, director of Agronomy

Sue Mecklenburg, vice president, Business Practices

Lauren Moore, director, Community Relations and Giving

Dave Olson, senior vice president, Culture and Leadership Development

Ben Packard, director, Environmental Affairs

May Snowden, vice president, Global Diversity

Brad Stevens, vice president, Marketing

Sandra Taylor, senior vice president, Corporate Social Responsibility

Peter Torrebiarte, general manager, Farmers Support Center, Costa Rica

193

Many other Starbucks executives and leaders participated in this book through meetings, telephone interviews, and other forms of support. These include, but are not limited to, Howard Schultz, Jim Alling, Carla Archambault, Paul Boardman, Tesh Burke, Dina Campion, Kevin Carothers, Odilia d'Aramon-Guepín, Jim Delehoy, Anne Ewing, Renny Freet, Omolla Gaya, Chris Gorley, Kristena Hart, Hiromitsu Hatta, Nerieda Hernandez, Dai Ichikawa, Gregg Johnson, Timothy Jones, Annette King, Kimberly Kelly, Gerald Kyle, Lisa Lenahan, Karen Mahoney, Leeann Mesa, Sheeba Oriko, Nancy Poznoff, Kathy Ragsdale, David Silldorff, Janeen Simmons, Orin Smith, Rich Soderberg, Jo Sorenson, Shelli Taylor, Amy Tingler, Holly Vanderknapp, Tom Walters, and Lara Wyss.

reader's guide

1. Try to distill *The Starbucks Experience* into a single sentence, and then discuss why that "experience" has led to such great success. Afterward, distill *your* company's "experience" into a single sentence and discuss ways it has led to your current level of success.

2. Apply the five key business principles of Starbucks to your business. Of the five principles, which one does your business most obviously embody and which one does your business most need to embrace? For example, does your business pay great attention to detail, following the edict that Everything Matters, and yet do little to Surprise and Delight your customers? Can you think of other principles, ones that your company strives to embody, that are not on the list?

3. Starbucks began with a question: "What if you took the quality coffee bean tradition and merged it with the charm and romance of the European coffeehouse?" Pose some "what if" questions about your own business that could lead to new products and services.

4. Much of the success of Starbucks derives from the sense of commitment to the corporate philosophy felt by the partners who work behind the counter. These partners are directly involved with customers and are, therefore, in a much better position to create loyalty and return business than are the corporate leaders. How does the

company achieve success in creating this commitment among its staff? What strategies has your company used to achieve this result? Which ones have worked, and which ones have failed? Which of the Starbucks strategies could your company implement most effectively to create a similar sense of commitment?

5. What do you think about Starbucks commitment to creating a positive, playful culture? How would you describe the culture of your company?

6. In Principle 1, Starbucks executive Howard Schultz is quoted as follows: "We are not in the coffee business serving people, but in the people business serving coffee. The equity of the Starbucks brand is the humanity and intimacy of what goes on in the communities. . . . The Starbucks environment has become as important as the coffee itself." Consider the benefit that your business truly is selling. Consider, too, the true nature of your brand equity. The book offers many examples of how the Starbucks leadership uses this sense of mission and brand equity to guide important decisions. How can you apply your new understanding of your mission and brand equity to one upcoming decision facing your company?

7. Starbucks partners are given a pound of coffee per week to take home, affording them a chance to use the product as customers use it. Do your company's employees use your products as customers use them? If not, think of ways you can make this happen.

8. Consider that the Starbucks business model calls for spending more on employee training than on advertising. As a result, it enjoys an excellent rate of employee retention and thereby continues the connection between

its partners and customers. How much does your business spend on training and advertising? Are these rates working well for your business? Can you apply the Starbucks model to achieve greater success?

9. Starbucks Five Ways of Being form a cornerstone of the company's service philosophy. But note that the company goes beyond simply providing its partners with the list. Instead, through the *Green Apron Book*, partners learn specific methods for applying the Ways of Being. In what way does your company present its philosophies? How could they be presented in more active ways?

10. Attention to detail is a key factor in the success of Starbucks and of many other companies. How well is your company handling even the smallest details on a daily basis? In what ways is your company a role model for other companies? Or are there areas where you can improve this facet of your business?

11. Look at your business through the lens of the following statement from Principle 2: "[E]very company's brand is nothing more than the sum total of the actions its people take." Considered through this lens, what is your brand identity, and which actions have most strongly shaped it? What future actions can continue to shape it in a positive way?

12. In Principle 2, you read that an unwillingness to compromise quality impeded the growth of Starbucks for many years. Packaging technology did not exist to ensure a fresh product throughout a large geographic area. That same commitment to a quality product eventually led to tremendous success. Consider the shortcuts your company feels are necessary. How do they affect the bottom

line? How do they affect the brand itself? What are the long-term risks and rewards? Which ones can you eliminate to ensure a higher-quality product and greater brand reputation?

13. Nearly all companies claim to pride themselves on quality service, but the Starbucks mandate to "surprise and delight" goes a step further. Rather than seeking just to meet your customers' needs, are there ways your product or service can go to the next step by providing a uniquely positive experience that will create stronger brand loyalty?

14. Recall negative feedback you have received recently. What was the source? A customer? A colleague? How did you react? Did you thank the person for taking time to point out the problem, or did you deny the validity of the complaint and leave the problem unresolved? How could you have handled the situation differently? Does your company tend to welcome complaints and respond? Does your company, to use *The Starbucks Experience* phrase, "embrace resistance"?

15. How adaptable is your company? Cite some examples to support your response. Do the company leaders show flexibility in their approach to problems, seeking positive solutions? Note the statement in Principle 4: "At times great leadership is little more than making sound compromises." What do you think about that statement? How does it apply to your company's leadership?

16. What do you think about Starbucks belief that environmental responsibility should be a corporate value? Why

does the company measure its performance with a "triple bottom line"?

17. As a result of the many recent corporate scandals, we all hear a lot of talk about the lack of social responsibility in the corporate world. Discuss your thoughts about corporate social responsibility (CSR). As this book suggests, CSR is "about developing a reputation of integrity so there is trust with employees, investors, customers, suppliers, and their communities." Reflect on the level of trust your company inspires in each of these groups. Are there ways you can strengthen that trust?

18. What strategies in the book do you find most easily adaptable to your business? What steps can you take to put these strategies in place right away? How will your coworkers feel about implementing these strategies? What ongoing concerns would these strategies resolve?

19. What strategies that have worked for Starbucks would *not* work for your business? Explain the reasons why you feel this way.

20. Choose an anecdote in the book—perhaps the one you feel is most instructive or most memorable—and use it to illustrate a feeling you have about your company or to illustrate a point within your overall approach to business.

index

about the author

Dr. Joseph Michelli is an organizational psychologist who has dedicated his career to studying successful businesses, both large and small. Prior to *The Starbucks Experience*, Dr. Michelli coauthored *When Fish Fly: Lessons for Creating a Vital and Energized Workplace* with John Yokoyama the owner of the World Famous Pike Place Fish Market in Seattle.

Dr. Michelli transfers his knowledge of exceptional business practices through keynote addresses and workshops. These presentations provide ways to develop playful and productive workplaces that maximize productivity while fueling growth and employee morale.

In addition to his dynamic and entertaining international keynote presentations, Dr. Michelli and his staff provide

- CEO consultation
- Corporate coaching
- Leadership team development services
- Group facilitation and team-building strategies
- Individual development planning
- Creation of open management systems
- Customized management and frontline training programs

For additional complimentary resources concerning *The Starbucks Experience*, please visit: www.josephmichelli.com.

Dr. Michelli is eager to help you to bring *The Starbucks Experience* fully to life in your business. He can be reached through his Web site, email at joseph@josephmichelli.com, or by calling either (719) 473-2414 or 888-711-4900.

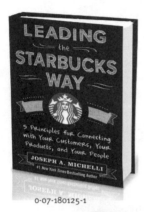